Praise for *Even Monkeys F* D0005544

"*Even Monkeys Fall From Trees* brings a refreshing message and a holistic approach to customer service. In a masterful, yet practical way, Doug Lipp gives us a formula for balancing the science of technical ability and the art of interpersonal skills. It is more fun to be swinging in the trees, but falling is just a reminder to get our life in balance. What a valuable learning! Doug invites us to take care of ourselves so that we can delight and care for our customers."

— Jeanette Haas, RSM
Senior Vice President of Mission Services
Owensboro Mercy Health System

"Doug Lipp has taught customer service to some of the largest and most prestigious companies in the world. By following the customer service principles laid out in *Even Monkeys Fall From Trees*, I have secured some of the largest Japanese investments in the United States. I enjoyed this book, particularly the references to Disney. I think the subtitle should be something along the lines of 'don't wait until you lose a major client to buy this book.'"

— Al Gianini, Managing Director
CB Richard Ellis

"Doug's unique philosophy towards the science and art of customer service is timeless and applicable to all industries at all levels . . . it is a refreshing change from the usual. From receptionist to CEO, his techniques can help you win the war of customer service."

— Eric Frasier, V. P., National Sales Manager
Conseco Fund Group

"This book provided common sense solutions to help everyone at all levels of the organization. The exercises 'The Seven Absolutes' will be especially useful as training tools for my customer service organization. The material is innovative and creative, yet practical. The scenarios are realistic, allowing workers to visualize themselves in similar circumstances."

— Donna Hatcher, Customer Service Manger
NEC Electronics

About this book

"Good evening to all of you and welcome to our annual all employee meeting. I am sorry to inform you that, in spite of the superior performance of our products, the numbers before you tell the awful truth. We have answered the call of our competitors by improving product quality. But we have lost every one of our premium accounts, our client turnover is 100% for the year. Why? Because we haven't taken the time to contact our clients and tell them we appreciate their business. We leave them in the dark instead of giving them regular updates on changes in our industry. They feel ignored and are tired of it. These aren't my words but the words of our ex-customers."

Sound familiar to you? These comments were recently made by a senior executive at a meeting of nearly 700 sales and service professionals. The company? A household name. Anyone who has ever invested a dollar of their savings on Wall Street or watched a few hours of television knows it well. Their problem? They, like thousands of other organizations large and small, are *out of balance*. They put all of their eggs in the product quality and technology basket and forgot the interpersonal needs of their customers. Unique? Not a bit. But, this is not to say that technology is bad and interpersonal stuff is good; it is simply a matter of equilibrium. It would be equally disastrous for a company to focus on developing nice employees at the expense of product quality, reliability, or availability.

In the past 25 years, customer service has been alternately hailed as the magic bullet for business success or derided as just another "management program." After being bombarded with books, speeches, videos, training sessions, magazine articles, and more, customer service is a subject with which we are intimately familiar. Many organizations and corporations have taken great strides to improve and maintain outstanding quality and service, some with outstanding success. The quality service drive got its start in the 1970s after we realized the Japanese were cleaning our plow with better products. To combat this, we embraced the notion of Quality Control Circles, expanding to Total Quality Management and Statistical Process Control in the 1980s and 1990s. As a result, organizations made great progress in improving the quality of many products and services. Many of us have come to know and respect names of people and organizations synonymous with the push for quality. Statistical process control gurus Edwards Deming and Dr. Joseph M. Juran, ISO 9000, and the Malcolm Baldridge Award are well known and respected.

And yet, in spite of the thousands of dollars, and countless hours spent on improving service and quality, there is still something missing from the customer service approaches of many businesses . . . a lack of balance. The ability to provide outstanding customer service is as much an "art" as it is a "science." The art of customer service appeals to the emotional needs and ego of the customer. The scientific side consists of the ability to provide technical information, quality products and support. Both are necessary, but many companies are terribly skewed to one side or the other of this balance and the results are similar to the scenario listed above . . . lost business.

Even Monkeys Fall From Trees is designed to be a practical tool to help you analyze the service and products you or your organization provide from the standpoint of being in balance. How well are you attending to both the "art" and "science" needs of your employees and customers? Read a section, then do one of the **11 exercises** that have been adopted by world class organizations. By the end of the book, you will know the following:
1)   Your individual and organizational strengths,
2)   Where you need to make improvements,
3)   Specific action steps to maximize your strengths and minimize your weaknesses
. . . a blueprint to attain and maintain your balance!

Even Monkeys Fall From Trees

Even Monkeys Fall From Trees

The Balance of Art and Science for
Outstanding Customer Service

Doug Lipp
Hickethier Press International

www.douglipp.com

Front Cover Design: David Bradshaw
Typography by E. W. Enterprises

Sixth Printing 2012

ISBN: 978-0-9707648-0-5

Acknowledgments

Family unity is my source of life balance. Without their warmth and love, I wouldn't be able to work, travel, write, or live the life I have been blessed with. I thank each of you and dedicate this book to you.

• To my wife Pam. Thank you for being my life and business partner. You understand me. You create the support, the motivation, and the safety net I need to venture out and take risks.

• To our three children, Allison, Amanda and Keith. Thank you for sharing me with so many people and for being such great people and good buddies.

• To my parents, Gordon and Polly. Thank you for being the bedrock of support for the whole Lipp clan.

• To my sister Lorrie, my brother-in-law Dave, and my niece Carrie. Thank you for bringing laughter into my life.

I also want to thank others who have served as a source of inspiration and support.

•My friends and my fellow camp counselors at the Nagoya, Japan YMCA. They provided the friendship and support when I lived so far from home. In particular, Jun, Yoshie, and Michiru Akishige, who welcomed me into their family. I am eternally grateful and value our friendship to this day.

• Diana and Clint Stark for their counsel and understanding.

• Etta Worthington for her editing and production assistance. I truly appreciated her patience, wit, and ability to turn my words into something worth reading.

• Gini Scott, who helped bring structure and order to this book and served as a great sounding board in the early stages of the project.

Table of Contents

A Note from the Author

I first encountered the concept of maintaining balance in life as a graduate student at International Christian University (ICU) in Tokyo, Japan. I enrolled in the program because I wanted to master the Japanese language. In high school I had started studying Japanese. I loved it so much, I made it my minor in college. And now, I intended to become an expert, through immersion in both Japanese language and culture.

When I flew to Tokyo, I dove into the program immediately. My plans included a blistering pace of study so I could absorb as much as possible as quickly as I could. I shunned other foreign students at ICU. I didn't want to hear a word in English. And of course I wasn't going to speak it. I informed my Japanese roommates at the boarding house I wanted nothing to do with English. No built-in English tutor. I considered our living area an "English-free zone." I was there to learn Japanese!

I aced the classes my first semester. A real success. Time to turn up the heat. I decided to tackle the most advanced Japanese-language class taught at the university. Within weeks, I was dragging myself out of bed early to finish homework. Every day all day I was working—working on my assignments, working to excel. Hours spent memorizing new vocabulary words. Hours learning how to read and write the complicated Japanese alphabet called Kanji. I was totally immersed. And I was in over my head.

Every free moment I studied. I rushed out of classes, no time to socialize with other Japanese students on campus. No time to explore the country I had come to live in. But I wasn't happy. I had flown 5,000 miles, left family and friends, to study and savor a culture I loved. But I wasn't enjoying it. I had no time for the richness of the Japanese culture I had dreamed of absorbing. It wasn't much different from living in the United States, scuttling from classroom to library to dormitory room.

I got more and more discontent but I couldn't admit it. That would mean that I was wrong or had failed. That was unacceptable. I'd always excelled at Japanese studies back home. Always studied hard, been at the top of my class in both high school and college. But this was different. I felt like a failure.

One day during a lecture in one of my more difficult classes, I started to feel anxious. The material was much more complex than what I was ready for. And the homework assignment promised hours and hours of hard work . . . if I could complete it successfully! Suddenly my stomach began to cramp. I clutched my abdomen as waves of nausea swept over me.

The pain wouldn't leave. I dashed out of class, hopped on my bicycle, and pedaled back to my boarding house. I rushed in the door and down the hall to the bathroom. I vomited. And then I noticed—there was blood in the vomit.

I had a problem. I was clearly way out of balance and I

had to do something. I couldn't go on like this. I had to change something so I could benefit from my months in Japan instead of hating them. The next day I marched over to the university administrative offices and dropped the class. I took a deep breath and then I joined the Aikido Club, which was open to all students. Aikido is one of many martial arts. Aikido attracted me because of its emphasis on balance, and on inner peace, as a means of handling attackers.

Three hours each time the club met we would focus on Aikido. But the three-hour workout turned out to be only one! The first hour we meditated. And after only one hour of physical workout, we meditated for another hour.

I was the only non-Japanese member of the club, probably the only member fretting about this terrible waste of time. I was there to learn Aikido. But two thirds of the time I sat on the floor in silence, involved in my own inner world. This was exactly what I needed. But it was hard for me as a Westerner to embrace.

Fortunately, the Aikido instructor noticed my discomfort and took extra time with me. Faithfully he would explain the Aikido philosophy after each practice session. I learned eventually. I understood. The goal of Aikido was not to forcefully control an attacker with counterpunches or kicks, but to use the energy of the attacker against him to neutralize his force.

"Why fight force with force?" my instructor would caution me. "If you push too hard, you will lose your balance and fall over."

Slowly I melted into this wisdom. I knew that feeling all too well. I was now ready to learn.

As we meditated, our instructor would lead us through

a number of mental exercises visualizing any number of attackers and how, by being relaxed, we could be more effective in neutralizing them. The attackers we visualized were not limited to people, menacing men on dark streets. As we sat mute and blind, our instructor pulled our minds to other attackers: school projects and the personal challenges that lay in wait for us.

First we practiced relaxing our muscles. We went through deep-breathing techniques. Each session started this way.

Early in our training, our instructor had demonstrated the power of relaxation. "Line up," he ordered. One by one he told us to prepare for his attack. One by one we braced, tried to keep him from pushing us over. And one by one we failed, pushed aside like paper dolls in the wind. We were no match for him.

"You tense up," he admonished us, "instead of relaxing." In our tense state we were totally out of balance and easy to push over.

He led us through another round of relaxation exercises and then lined us up again. This time the results were different. Each of us was able to deflect his blows and energy. In our relaxed states, we were much harder to push over. He had made his point clear. Now what he had told us made sense. "A balanced, relaxed mind and body are much more flexible and resilient than a tense mind and body that is out of balance and thus better able to handle attacks."

I pedaled slowly back to the boarding house that day, knowing I had learned something on a very deep level. It was something that would be very important to me. I understood what this was all about. *Balance = Strength.* This imprinted itself in my brain like a mathematical formula.

Balance = Strength. I knew it was right.

Years have passed, but I regularly flash on the significance of that lesson. I don't usually face physical attackers. Not many of us do. Most of my attackers actually appear in the form of self-doubt or uncertainty. When I remember the words of my wise instructor, I relax. And when I relax I am fully prepared for anything. When I am relaxed I fare much better because I can deal with challenges creatively and flexibly.

I think about the time when I had a long and stressful commute from my office to my home, some 15 years after graduating from college. I would trudge into the house and my children would immediately rush to me. "Daddy, can you help me with my homework?" Or another would ask me to play with him and his Legos.

"Not now," I'd usually bark at them. "I need some space."

I was in no mood to be bothered and would march off to change my clothes. I realized that my behavior was completely out of line and that I had forgotten the fundamentals of being in balance that I had learned so many years ago. But what to do?

I vowed to regain my balance daily before entering my house. Before pulling into my driveway, I would actually stop my car in front of my neighbor's house, several houses away, and practice some of the stress-reducing exercises I had learned so long ago. I would visualize myself in a relaxed state, free of the worries from work and crazy drivers. I also made sure I told my neighbor what I was doing! The point is that my five-minute relaxation break worked. I was much more relaxed as I pushed open the door to my home. My family deserved as much, if not more attention than I had given my colleagues and customers during the day!

What does this have to do with customer service? Everything! Remember, balance = strength, and as a service provider, you have many opportunities to address issues of balance regarding your product line, your management style, or how you interact with co-workers. I can't transport you back to my Aikido class of years ago. But I hope the ideas and activities introduced in this book help you and your work group achieve a sense of balance and strength.

Introduction

Even monkeys fall from trees. This is an old Japanese proverb that's a favorite of mine. It means that regardless of how capable or skilled we are, sooner or later, we all lose our balance and make mistakes. You've probably never seen a monkey fall from a tree, even at the zoo. I haven't either. But we've all seen remarkably capable people and even successful companies make mistakes—in other words, fall from their trees.

Admit it. You've probably dropped out of a few trees yourself and had to pick yourself up and see how you were. I have too. Think about it. How and when did these mistakes happen? What skill or ability are you most proud of? Now, stop for a moment and think about when you didn't use that skill or ability and didn't perform up to your standards, or when you let yourself and/or others down. That's the time when you "fell from the tree."

If you're like me, such memories aren't fun. However, these situations are ones you can learn a lot from. Think over what you did, how and why you made the mistake. From this you can make corrections so you won't repeat the mistake. You may need to ask yourself some questions to identify what caused the problem in the first place. Was it your lack of knowledge? Or was it how you reacted to others? Also, if you were able to remedy the situation, what behaviors or strategies helped your recovery?

Most likely, your "fall" didn't occur in isolation. Probably others observed it and reacted in some way. Most probably your "fall" affected others or at least drew some sort of response from co-workers. Think about it now (however unpleasant that may be). How did your co-workers react? How did you respond to them? Did you remove yourself from the situation and then take care of the problem later? Or did you think on your feet and remedy the situation in front of others?

Be honest now. Were you willing to own up to your own responsibility for the mistake? If so, you can pat yourself on the back. This is a key step in remedying the situation. Unfortunately, some companies and some individuals refuse to take responsibility for their failures. They blame the customer. They blame the market for the decline in market share or profits.

That's kind of like the monkey blaming the weak branch of a tree for a fall, instead of admitting it lost its balance. On the other hand, when you excel, you maintain your balance. Think about when you or others in your organization excelled. What did you do and how? Answering these questions will help you repeat your success.

In this book, I take the concept of learning from successes and mistakes—or the idea of keeping your balance in the trees—and apply it to customer service. You can learn from anything, whether it's your really good days or the days when you really bottom out. On the great days—those are the ones when you feel like you can do absolutely anything, nothing seems to phase you—you can provide outstanding service to your customers, even the most demanding ones. But then there are the other days. Days when you have trouble even getting out of bed. Days when you don't feel very willing or able to deal with those demanding customers.

You know by now that's part of the customer service game. Nobody can be a customer service robot. Always on, always charming, always polite. Sometimes being human gets in the way. And everyone makes mistakes. Those customers mentioned in the book include more than your external customers. Those people who buy your product or services. Your customers can be internal as well. These are you co-workers, your managers, and your subordinates.

Central to this book are the principles of staying in balance and of learning from your successes and mistakes to dramatically improve the quality of service you provide your customers. In this book, you'll find a process for improving the quality of service. There are exercises to do, either in workgroup sessions or by yourself.

The best way to use this book is to first read the book on your own. Then analyze your approach to customer service. Whether you are the CEO of a company, a mid-level manager, or a front-line employee—reading this book and doing the exercises will make you consider your current approach so you can identify both your strengths and the areas in which you need improvement.

After you've worked through things yourself, encourage others in your company or work group to do the same. That's easy if you're a manager. If you're a front-line employee, you can try and influence others to look into this book and use the ideas. You can use this grass-roots approach to encourage other groups to work through the exercises, then apply the principles within their group. With the success of one group, it will be easier to convince others to apply these principles in their work groups or throughout the company. The amazing power of this approach is connected to bringing together the work group to analyze issues as a group. It doesn't matter if the work unit is two or 200 people. The key to sustaining successful change is a group discussion of the issues. Then you'll need to practice effective approaches for your whole team, and to commit yourself to continual improvement of your customer service.

Use these principles regularly, diligently, and you'll find yourself falling out of the trees less often. And when you do make a mistake or fall due to a problem, you'll successfully handle the situation and recover quickly. And soon again you'll be swinging in the trees, maintaining your balance.

Just Remember Two Things

It's really quite simple. Staying in balance in customer service depends on just two factors. These two basic and essential elements for providing a successful balance of outstanding customer service are:

1. Technical Ability
2. Interpersonal Ability

These two elements are often overlooked even though the market is deluged with material on customer service techniques. Many organizations have been attacking this issue of quality customer service. And many have found success. For example, many manufacturers have expedited product delivery and have produced products that are cheaper, more durable, and of higher quality.

But I've seen some disturbing developments. Many service providers still ignore the need to balance technical and interpersonal ability. And these two elements are not strange or surprising. In fact, they are common sense.

With technical ability you know your job completely, you understand your company's products and services, and you are aware of the company policies and procedures. With this technical ability you can be knowledgeable and helpful. You thoroughly understand the science of customer service.

Having interpersonal ability means you've commanded a good understanding of and ability to use appropriate communication skills with your customers. With this interpersonal ability, you're certainly prepared to be courteous and friendly and you'll be providing what is known as the art of customer service.

In this book, I'll be discussing both the science and the art of customer service and how you as a customer service representative or a manager can master these.

Sounds like common sense, doesn't it? And it's true. But why doesn't everyone in customer service get it? Why don't we see consistently excellent customer service? Why is there a breakdown? The answer is balance. Many people, maybe even most people, don't know how to balance the technical side of their job with the interpersonal, both of which are qualities necessary to interact successfully with the customer. Many people aren't aware of the distinctions between the two parts of the job or they don't know how to apply them to satisfy customers. But the bottom line is this: if you want to provide high quality customer service, you're going to need to blend in just the right amount of technical knowledge with a good mix of interpersonal ability. And if you do this, you'll both meet and/or exceed your customer's expectations. And this is the hallmark of exceptional service. This is what we all strive for. And the key to arriving at this is a thorough understanding of these two basic elements of customer service.

You can analyze the quality of your customer service approach. Check the current state of both your technical and your interpersonal abilities. Are you quite skilled in the technical side of your job, but uncomfortable with dealing with people? Or are you what they call a people person, but you don't totally understand the technical aspects of your job? Maybe you can do both, but you are inconsistent in your performance. Doing both well consistently is what separates superb service providers from mediocre ones. This is never more true than when you deal with difficult situations, when you have a concerned, frightened, or even hostile customer. This book will help you develop strategies to deal with the challenges unique to your industry, the product or service you provide and your organization. And this is critical to successfully providing customer service.

Since this book is not just for the individual, I invite you to examine the effectiveness of your support group. You're not in it alone, although you may feel like it sometimes. You can't effectively provide good service, no matter how well you maintain a good balance, if the groups you rely on don't do their part. You know this, of course. The sales staff can't succeed if the factory is poorly run and products don't arrive on time. No matter how good your interpersonal skills or your product knowledge, you will lose customers if what you are selling is shoddy and doesn't meet customer needs.

While reading this book, you'll want to look beyond your own abilities and scrutinize the systems in your company. Do they enhance or detract from your ability to provide consistently excellent customer service.

Regardless of your business or your position in your organization, or whether you deal with external or internal customers, clients, or accounts, this book will give you what you need to provide great customer service.

Start with the exercises. Use these and the questionnaires to assess the state of your customer service balance. Once you find areas of needed improvement, make the commitment to change. With this book, you'll be able to answer honestly some basic questions such as:

- How flexible am I to the needs of my customers?
- Do I know what my customers expect and can I provide that and even more?
- How often do I surprise my customers with extra services they don't expect?
- Do I have a system in place to identify and remedy problems before they occur?

You can deal with your own limitations, and make changes you need to make. If you are a supervisor or manager, this book will help you look at your whole work group and give you ideas on how to implement change. If you are a front-line employee, consider introducing some of the exercises to your work team. Ideally, an entire work unit, from top to bottom will read the book and work on issues in a collaborative fashion. It is natural for managers and employees to have different perspectives and sources of concern and the strongest teams are able to share their mutual concerns and strategies for resolution. But you too can influence customer service quality in your company by example and by appropriately made suggestions for change within the company.

As you read though this text, keep in mind the proverb *Even monkeys fall from trees.* You'll be reflecting on how you and your team members, the management, and company employees respond to situations when you "fall from the customer service tree" and thereafter have to rush to do damage control. Once this happens, you have one of two directions to take:

A. You can stay on the ground after that. Blame others for your fall. Never admit the problems. Never recover from the fall. Or,

B. You can leap back up to the tree by admitting the problems and using feedback from customers and co-workers to keep you in balance out on those limbs. You can stay up in the tree even longer as you try to provide even better service. You can discover yourself more firmly balanced when the next challenge comes your way.

The choice is yours, which path will you take?

Part 1

The Balance of Art and Science

EVEN MONKEYS FALL FROM TREES

You rush into the grocery store on your way home from the office. You just need a few things. Of course you get in the line where there's a price check which seems to last forever. The checker is quite pleasant. He chats with the customer. Compares notes about a friend they have in common. When the price is verified, he continues his conversation and methodically completes the checkout, showing no signs of hurry. He even helps the packer perched at the end of his checkout line, and waves at the customer when she leaves.

If you're the second, or third, or fourth person in the line, you don't really appreciate this checker's customer service. Was he friendly? You bet, but he was ignoring the needs of the other customers waiting in line. He wasn't efficient.

Or you may grab the phone and dial a tech support line when you are installing new software on your computer. The three minute automated maze of getting to a real person leaves you a little anxious. Then you hear a live voice. You explain your problem. He cuts you off before you're finished. His tone says, "Is this woman stupid, or what!" You grit your teeth and ask your other questions. His answers are clipped.

"Can I stay on the line while I try to boot up the program again?"

"Call back if it doesn't work. It will if you've done everything correctly."

The line is dead. You try. It works. You're partly relieved but still smarting from the insinuation of inadequacy by the tech advisor. Was he efficient and accurate? You bet, but he wasn't friendly. He answered the immediate problem. But you're still not sure why it happened. You worry about what will happen if you ever need to reinstall the program.

What happened in each of the above cases happens all too frequently. As consumers, we are subjected more and more to service providers who just don't seem to grasp the big picture of service. Being attentive, warm, and friendly doesn't have to result in slow or inefficient service. On the other hand, being technically competent doesn't give the service provider the right to be abrasive or insensitive.

It is a question of striking the service balance.

Chapter 1

The Balancing Act

Successful customer service needs—no—demands a balanced approach. Balancing the Science and Art of service gives you the ability to be flexible in how you approach each customer, based on that customer's needs and background. In other words, you are able to use a more scientific or technical approach with the customer who demands information and doesn't need a lot of emotional support or chit-chat. Likewise, for the customer who is concerned, confused, or upset, you will be able to choose a more artful or emotional approach.

When you are successfully balancing your approach to service, you also will be committed to accomplishing two critical goals:

- Increasing the joy of attention
- Eradicating the pain of neglect

Combining these positive goals of offering attention and avoiding neglect is fundamental to continued success, so it's important to learn the steps for providing both. Once you do, you'll offer outstanding, <u>consistent</u> service to your customers. There's no question. Anyone can provide great service from time to time, when motivated to pay special attention to a customer. The real success stories come from taking care of the details every day. These are the individuals and companies who provide great service on an ongoing basis. That means great service from the beginning to the end of the shift, outstanding service from one location to another, whether domestic or international.

You've Got to Be Balanced

Think of the delicate balance that must be attained in order to construct a sturdy wall of brick or stone. Too many bricks on one side or the other and you have a wall that will eventually fall over. Similarly, the essential building blocks for outstanding service involve creating a series of balances so that what you and your company have built won't teeter and fall. When you are in balance, you have a good chance of meeting and even exceeding your customers' expectations. Out of balance, though, you're in trouble! Like many individuals or companies, you will fail or slowly limp along. You won't be able to give your customers what they want. The result? Reduced customer demand.

To reach this needed balance, you'll have to combine both the interpersonal "art" and technical "science" of customer service. Use your heart or intuition to provide the art of customer service. This appeals to the emotional and ego needs of your customer. Use your head to gather and understand the necessary information to provide the scientific side. This depends on market and product research findings and your ability to provide technical information and support. Mix the art and science together, and you've got great customer service—a combination of excellent, high quality products and great service which supports the products.

This is the formula for success:

Excellent product

+ *Balance of Art and Science*

= *Customer Satisfaction*

The Balance of Art and Science

Let's look a little more closely at those two sides that must be kept in balance.

ART	SCIENCE
• Emotion	• Technical Knowledge
• Attitudes	• Skills
• Intuition	• Research Findings
• Heart	• Sufficient Quantity of Product
• Quality of Interaction	• Knowledge of Systems and Policies

EXCELLENT PRODUCT

By providing customers with a balanced combination of the qualities listed above, you'll be offering outstanding customer service. When you can master both sides, you combine exhibiting a concern for you customer's needs—the "art" of customer service—with your ability to do something about those needs—the "science" of customer service. In essence, you are able to do the two things listed earlier: provide the joy of attenton and reduce the pain of neglect.

Be warned! If there's a breakdown at any place in this balanced system, the result is the pain of neglect. This is the hallmark of poor customer service. Think of it this way:

Marginal Product and/or

No Balance of Art and Science

= Pain of Neglect

= Customer Dissatisfaction

Finding the Right Art and Science Balance

Unfortunately, just knowing this idea doesn't mean you've mastered it. It's not so easy to find the right art and science balance, even when you know the mechanics of balancing the emotional and informational components that make up good service. That's because the art of providing outstanding service is by its nature very elusive and diffi-

8

cult to teach and learn, simply because it is an "art."

What do you think of when you hear the word art? Maybe you think of subjectivity, of hazy lines and definitions. This art of customer service is made up of "soft" intangible elements. These depend on a number of subjective criteria—from your own style and personality to the personal style, culture, and needs of your customer. To make it even more difficult, you have to balance these soft subjective qualities against the science or "hard" elements of customer service to achieve the right mix. What is the right mix? Well, the answer is one that most of us are not usually very comfortable with—that there isn't always an exact right or wrong answer. Sometimes the answer is "it depends."

Here's a good way to think of this distinction: the soft side takes care of the customer's emotional needs, while the hard side takes care of the customer's informational needs as summarized in the chart below.

Customer Needs

		For Information	For Emotional Support
Type of Service	Hard (Science)	Good Match	Too Much Science
	Soft (Art)	Too Much Art	Good Match

As this hard/soft, science/art distinction illustrates, you need both sides to deliver outstanding service. The hard or science side of things tends to be easier to grasp. The soft/art qualities are much more difficult to teach or learn, because they are so personal, subjective, and situational. But keep working with them. You'll gradually develop more of a feel for what works and what doesn't under different circumstances. It's intuitive, a "yeah, I got it" process.

Even though these soft qualities are hard to teach and learn, you absolutely must develop this skill. No matter how much you know about your product, service, company, or whatever, you won't be fully effective if you haven't mastered the art side of customer service. A salesperson who knows everything anyone might want to know about the product but doesn't smile or treat customers with respect will be as ineffective as the super-friendly salesperson who is easy to talk to but can't answer a customer's vital technical questions about the product.

Think about any poor customer service you have observed or experienced. Quite simply, the two primary reasons for being ineffective are these:

1) The service provider is out of balance and overusing either the science or art of service.

2) There isn't a good match between what the customer wants and the response of the service provider.

No matter who your customer is, if your approach is too information-oriented and sort of robotic, and lacks emotion, you will be perceived by customers as uncaring and mechanical. On the other hand, if you rely primarily on courtesy and friendliness over job or product knowledge, customers may consider you unknowledgeable, or worse yet, incompetent.

You cannot choose one approach over the other. You must be good at using both and knowing the appropriate times to use them. If not, an imbalance in either direction can lead to disaster. Any employee who is out of balance in either direction won't be effective, whether dealing with external customers or internal ones (such as other employees).

Examples of Being Out Of Balance

Too Much Art

• She's perky. She friendly. Got a great sense of humor. "Where are the results of the market research we ran last week?" you ask the administrative assistant. Her blank expression answers you. You shake your head and tromp down the hall to her boss. To complain. Again.

• You like him. He never complains about staying late to work on your car. You come back with the same problem after he's already "fixed" it and he's as pleasant as always. He works late. You drive off. But you still have the same problem. It's

Too Much Science

• If you want a straight answer you know who to go to. The accounting manager has all the answers. And you know they're the right answers. However, walking into his office is like facing the lions. He's curt and scowls at everyone who ventures near. As a result, no one likes him and he's an impossible team member.

• Then there's the department manager who seems to have memorized the company handbooks. Wonder about a company policy? He knows it. But he can't seem to see beyond those lists and

Too Much Art	*Too Much Science*
clear, he doesn't know how to fix it. And you've spent a bit of money and a lot of time but still have a malfunctioning car. • Everyone likes her. She's the manager who truly does have an open door policy. Everyone in the department is comfortable talking with her. They leave her office feeling listened to. But nothing really changes. Although she's good with her employees, she doesn't fight for them with her superiors. So policies that need to be changed are never changed. • He has been in the company forever. Knows the ins and outs of every bit of corporate history and the various product lines. He loves to chat and is the life of every department activity. He even sends birthday cards to every employee in the department and is the first to	pages of policy. His department is made up of people from a wide variety of cultural backgrounds. He treats them all the same and according to the book. Cultural differences? He doesn't know they exist. This is most evident when he's providing coaching or critical feedback. His lack of cultural sensitivity creates a major dissatisfaction in the team. Everyone grumbles about him. • Call the 800 number and you know your call will be picked up within two rings. Every time. But the answer may be a harried customer service rep who barks out "hello." Or a sharp voice saying "Hold, please." And you hear music for three minutes while a mechanical voice assures you that your problem is important and that you will be serviced as soon as . . . The curt or nonex-

Too Much Art	*Too Much Science*
organize a potluck to celebrate something . . . anything. But just ask him to follow up with a client who has called with a question or a complaint. He is always too "busy" to take care of the people who pay the bills.	istent human beings in this customer service operation leave customers with their emotional needs unmet. The art side is overlooked, even though the phone is answered right away.

• He is brilliant in his field of expertise. No one questions this sales rep who knows every technical detail of his product. But he has an ego a mile high and you have to work with him. And dread it, just like everyone else in the company. He yells at anyone who gets in his way or who doesn't provide information instantly. Often his language is peppered with insults and expletives. Nobody likes to work with him. Nobody jumps to his aid when he needs support.

Certainly you can think of many more examples to illustrate what happens when there is an art/science imbalance. Again and again, these examples show the importance of achieving this critical state of balance.

How do you get to this state? The following sections describe the steps to learning the art and science of customer service and how to combine them. Then, you have to experiment and practice applying these techniques, so you can reach the proper art/science mix in your own situation with different kinds of customers under different circumstances.

Chapter 2

Practicing the "Art" of Customer Service

To some extent, the artistic, emotional side of service depends on your personality and style. But it is also made up of certain basic skills you can learn that are fundamental to outstanding customer service—courtesy, friendliness, and respect for your customers. The three basic skills are these:
- Active/Empathetic Listening
- Sincerity
- Ability to Apologize

They comprise the basics of the "ART" in the balance of art and science, as described in the customer satisfaction equation. We looked at this before but here's a view of the equation with the "ART" emphasized.

Excellent product

+ Balance of ART and Science

= Customer Satisfaction

These skills may be more natural for some individuals; for others, more difficult to learn. Doesn't matter where you stand, these skills can be learned. Don't disappear if these skills don't seem to come to you effortlessly. You can still achieve a high level of competence and comfort in using these skills if you work at it.

Suppose you aren't a natural empathetic listener. Maybe you like to do things quickly and don't like taking the time to listen to what you think you already know. Well, the good news is that you can learn to slow down. Maybe you feel uncomfortable apologizing because that shows weakness, and you have been brought up to always act like you are strong and in control. You can practice apologizing. Try a sincere "I'm sorry." This doesn't make you seem weak. Similarly, you can develop a genuine interest in and concern for your customers, so you really are sincere in your communication with them.

Let's look at how to develop each of these skills.

Active/Empathetic Listening

Focus and attention are what you need to become an active/empathetic listener. You want to show your concern and caring. You need to show you understand through empathy. When you have empathy, you see the world through the other person's eyes and look at his problem from his perspective. Here's an example: "I know you have been waiting for a long time and I appreciate your patience," you tell your customer, and say that you understand and care. Here you show empathy (we all know what it's like to be kept waiting) and then you give some emotional support. Through these words, you show (not just tell) that you really do understand the individual's feelings, even if you, as a service provider, have no control over the wait time.

To be an active/empathetic listener, listen closely and carefully to what the other person is saying and *how* the words are being said to get at the real meaning. In other words, you can get a more accurate picture of the emotional content of the speaker's words by paying attention to the mix of words, inflections, and body language. For example, an active/empathetic listener will be careful to observe the following areas when interacting with another person:

• the inflection (or the tone and texture) of the words,

• the person's body language (whether he is relaxed or tense, suggesting whether he is comfortable and satisfied or anxious and angry).

Together, these elements give you a clue as to how the person feels.

"I need help." This can have a number of meanings. Imagine this scenario. A customer trudges up to your counter. You look up and she says with a weak sigh, "I need help." This suggests she feels helpless and is seeking emotional support. Picture another customer marching up and leaning over your counter and nearly barking these words at you. "I need help." You probably get it. She is demanding attention and action right now to resolve an immediate concern rather than hearing words of reassurance and support before you take action.

Use active listening to determine exactly what your customers need, both by listening to what they say and do—the surface of their words and actions—and by noting the deeper meanings conveyed by those actions and words.

An empathetic approach can help you uncover those underlying meanings and show you really understand and care. When you sense a customer is really frustrated, share your perceptions, and probe for more insight into that customer's feelings.

"I bet you're really frustrated with this whole situation, and I certainly appreciate your patience. I want to help and make this work for you, so do you mind if I ask a couple of questions?"

The Wrong Way: Getting Defensive

Sometimes the best way to learn is by a bad example so here's what not to do. This is a defensive response. You attempt to justify, explain, or excuse what the customer is complaining about, rather than being open and receptive. Remember, these last two traits are the hallmarks of empathy.

She looked at the statement in the mail. Her stock portfolio was performing poorly, so Simone punched in the phone number for Hamid, her personal financial planner.

Simone: "What's going on down there? The stocks you put me in are real dogs. They've been performing terribly in recent months. And on top of that, you haven't kept in touch with me to let me know how they were doing, so we could discuss any changes in my portfolio. I am so frustrated I could scream."

Hamid (defensively): "Now Simone, you know I don't control the market. And from the very beginning, I never promised you double-digit returns. The market always changes. I think things will turn

18

around soon. I haven't called you since I have been going crazy trying to keep on top of this market lately. I have to spend my time looking for good deals for my clients and not calling them every day. You know I really am actively looking for good investment opportunities for you. I'll keep you better informed in the future."

You can see why this approach won't work very well. Most likely Simone would see this as an excuse, with Hamid explaining away the poor performance of the stocks he chose for her. To make matters worse, Hamid told her about his problems, but didn't address hers. This is a self-centered response—the exact opposite of empathy. His explanation was based on his own point of view as a long-time investment specialist used to the ups and downs of the stock market. His service to Simone was unbalanced. It was based on Science. He told Simone about the nature of the stock market. But as he was educating her, he completely ignored her needs for reassurance and support. He missed out on the Art side of the service equation when he didn't demonstrate empathy.

The Right Way: Listening with Empathy

Let's do an instant replay but change things a bit. Here's an example of the right way to respond, where you empathetically listen, apologize, and sincerely seek to make things right. Here's what could have happened given the same scenario.

She looked at the statement in the mail. Her stock portfolio was performing poorly, so Simone punched in the phone number for Hamid, her personal financial planner.

Simone: "What's going on down there? The stocks you put me in are real dogs. They've been performing terribly in recent months. And on top of that, you haven't kept in touch with me to let me know how they were doing, so we could discuss any changes in my portfolio. I am so frustrated I could scream."

Hamid: (with genuine concern): "You're absolutely right, Simone. Your investments haven't done as well as either of us anticipated, and I know you invested with my firm to avoid this type of volatility. And to make matters worse, I have been so involved in following the roller-coaster events of the market that I haven't kept you informed. I know how much you want to know what's happening. So if you have a moment now, I can tell you what I've been doing in the last few weeks to try to assess where the market will be going so I can better advise you. And then let's look at what a good strategy might be for you right now."

The key to the effectiveness of this more empathetic approach is that even though Simone's investments have fallen and haven't rebounded yet (there's nothing that can change that right at the moment), she feels listened to and her frustration has been validated. Instead of dumping Hamid for another broker, she might be willing to give him another chance. Through listening, he has cooled down the situation and showed how he could help by providing the Art side of the service balance. But now the pressure is on. He has to show he is equally skilled at the Science side of the business by advising her on how to improve her stock portfolio in order to keep her business.

As these contrasting scenarios illustrate, the ability to effectively listen to and communicate with your customers, especially those who are frustrated, is a vital tool on the Art side of the equation in your arsenal of outstanding customer service skills.

Sincerity

To show sincerity, you need to truly mean what you say—or at least back up your words with the actions, body language, and inflections which are congruent with your message. You need this consistency, since your words alone don't convey your intentions. It is the whole package you present the listener: *what* you are saying (your words) and *how* you say those words (your actions and tone of voice).

In fact, your tone of voice and body language generally carry a much stronger message than your words, since these come across as your true meaning. As the old adage goes, "Actions speak louder than words."

If your tone and body language reinforce your message, you will seem honest and truthful—in short, sincere. But if there is a discrepancy between your tone, your body language, and your words, customers will sense this and go away believing you to be insincere. They may suspect you are lying, being deceptive, concealing important information, covering up. They will think you are not really saying what you mean.

Think about this common phrase: "I'll be right with you." Say this in a warm, friendly, polite way, establishing eye contact, and smile. Your customer most likely will think you sincerely mean these words, particularly if you follow up in 30 seconds to a minute with an offer to help now. Done differently, (no eye contact or follow-up) these same words, "I'll be right with you," which have the potential to communicate a helpful, friendly offer, can ring hollow or insincere, particularly as the customer waits impatiently, feeling ignored. A much better, more sincere response would be to politely say, "I'll be with you in a minute or two, as soon as I'm finished with _____." (Fill in whatever you are doing.) But say "I'll be right with you," in a snappish, I'm-busy-don't-bother-me-way, and the customer will be convinced you are annoyed with him or her. There is a disconnect between what you are saying and doing. You are clearly being insincere.

So much depends on the tone of voice and body language that accompany your words. The same phrase can brand you as sincere or insincere. To have that sincere approach which is the hallmark of outstanding customer service, you need to support your words with a positive tone of voice and the appropriate positive body language. Use friendly gestures, smile, and look at your customer directly in a warm, cheerful manner.

Slight changes in your approach are the only difference between an effective or ineffective conversation. Consider the dramatic difference in the effects of these two approaches in the following examples.

The WRONG Way to Show Sincerity

You push your cart to the line at the grocery checkout stand with your cart. Your cashier is yakking to the cashier in the next lane about his weekend plans. As you plop your items onto the moving belt, your cashier grabs them and scans each one quickly, still carrying on his conversation. "It's $14.71," he informs you. "I have to see the new Mel Gibson movie. I have Saturday night off, so I'm going downtown to see it," he tells his co-worker. You toss down a 20 dollar bill. He pulls away from his conversation, looking annoyed, and says "Five twenty nine is your change. Have a good weekend." Before you can reply, he's turned his back on you and has grabbed the next customer's merchandise. You leave feeling annoyed, thinking the cashier incredibly rude.

The RIGHT Way to Be Sincere

Now imagine yourself going to a different grocery store. This time, as you approach the checkout stand, the two cashiers who had been talking stop promptly. Your cashier looks right at you and says, "Hello, how are you doing this afternoon?" As he scans your items, he comments on the nice weather expected for the weekend and takes your 20 dollar bill. Moments later, after he finishes ringing up your purchases, he hands you your change. Again he smiles broadly, "That's $5.29 back to you. Have a good weekend." You wish him the same and leave thinking about the friendly and quick service you got at that store.

Notice the Difference

Both clerks used the same parting phrase, "have a good weekend," but the difference is dramatic. In the first case, the clerk seems to be spouting the words mechanically, repeating something he has been instructed to say by a supervisor. Truth is, he really doesn't care. By contrast, the second clerk seems to genuinely hope you will have a great weekend. You can feel it in his attentive interest and smile. But he didn't overdo it. He balanced the interpersonal attention with efficiency and was on to the next customer without you feeling rushed.

Sincerity cannot be faked or glossed over. The real meaning, feelings, intentions, and interest shine through.

Think about exchanges you've had in the past with customer service providers. Perhaps a salesperson or waiter became extremely friendly and complimented you on your tie or scarf. But it was said so perfunctorily that you sensed intuitively he or she didn't care in the least. Something about his words didn't ring true, and you experienced him as a "sales robot"—a salesperson who says all the right pleasant things, but doesn't truly feel them.

Or maybe it was the saleswoman in the clothing store who said when you left, "Y'all come back now" without looking you in the eyes. You noticed the discrepancy, because there is a real difference between being sincere and faking it. You can recognize when someone is being insincere, because there is a disconnect between the words, gestures, tone of voice, and energy behind these words and actions. If you pay attention, you can notice this disconnect. Many customers do. That's because people believe the actions they see first. Second they believe the other person's tone of voice, and lastly, the words they choose. As soon as they sense a disconnect between the words, actions, or tone of voice, they immediately distrust those words. By contrast, they sense sincerity when all three elements are saying the same thing.

The Ability to Apologize

The third fundamental skill you need to successfully practice the art of customer service is the ability to apologize. You need to master phrases like "I'm sorry," "I made a mistake," "I apologize," or otherwise admit when you are wrong. Sometimes you even need to admit being wrong when you aren't, but when the customer is convinced that you are. Roger Fisher and William Ury point out the power of the apology in their best-selling book on negotiation, *Getting to Yes*: "On many occasions an apology can defuse emotions effectively, even when you do not acknowledge personal responsibility for the action or admit an intention to do harm. An apology can be one of the least costly and most rewarding investments you can make."

It is often very difficult to apologize, however, and there are several reasons.

1) This is because in American culture, saying "I'm sorry" or "I apologize" means that you are admitting being personally at fault or having made a mistake or error.

2) Another reason is that, quite frankly, in the world of customer service, there are many times when the person dealing with the upset customer isn't personally at fault, so the feeling is "why should I apologize—I didn't make the mistake!"

3) Or we can't admit error, because we associate making mistakes with negligence and legal liability, although most mistakes hardly rise to that danger. We buy into popular expressions that reflect these ideas, such as "never say you're sorry" or "never admit failure." These make any acknowledgment of error even more difficult.

Consequently, words of apology rarely pass through the lips of most service providers. Even if a customer service rep is inclined to say "sorry," the legal departments of many companies dissuade the practice due to liability fears. This reluctance to apologize is unfortunate, because an apology can defuse a situation. This can make all the difference in a customer feeling good and overcoming angry feelings when there is a problem. Often this willingness to apologize and appeal to the consumer's understanding has even fore-stalled legal suits, reduced damage claims, or resulted in more customers after the mistake is corrected.

A prime example of this was the McNeil Division of the Johnson & Johnson Company. When a crank tampered with several Tylenol medicine bottles in 1982, the company did a masterful job of regaining consumer confidence. They jumped to assume responsibility for a product tampering scandal (which wasn't even their fault). Similarly, in 1997, when the Odwalla Juice Company faced a crisis they took responsibility. Some consumers got sick from apple juice tainted with the E.coli bacteria, a problem caused by not pasteurizing their juices. Addressing the problem quickly, they were able to regain consumer confidence after they announced a change in their processing method. They achieved this result with their balanced approach. First they appealed to their customers' soft, interpersonal needs for reassurance and quick, direct action. Then they took care of their customers' hard, technical needs for better product preparation by developing a new "flash pasteurization" process which killed E.coli bacteria without compromising the nutritional quality of the beverage.

When you work with customers in any sales or service situation and a problem occurs, a *sincere* apology has magical powers to defuse tense situations and calm the customer. No matter whether you are directly responsible for the problem or whether it's due to the system, equipment failure, or even an overly demanding, impatient customer—a heartfelt, sincerely-expressed apology can go a long way to placate the customer and resolve the problem. Try "I'm sorry you had to wait so long, how can I help you?" or "I apologize for the confusion; let me help." These phrases are extremely effective.

Should things go wrong resulting in an upset customer, take the attitude of "Don't fight. Make it right." This will not only help you resolve the current situation, but it will contribute to satisfied customers. Customers will keep coming back since you've made what was wrong right. You've succeeded at providing great customer service. And you've retained a customer.

Failing to Apologize: The Consequences
Consider this case of the apology that never came. And the result.

Roger was excited. He was going to go hiking on his vacation. He needed some special camping equipment. Pouring over catalogs, he found just the items he needed. When he called to order the three items he wanted, only ten days remained before he was to leave.

"Will the order get here in time for my hiking trip?" he asked.

"All the items are in stock," the salesperson assured him. "We'll ship the order tomorrow. Should arrive in three to five days."

Roger was satisfied and continued his preparations for the trip. By the seventh day, the order still hadn't arrived and Roger was worried. Would the order arrive in the next three days so he would have them for his trip?

To check, he called the customer service department with his order number and the customer service rep dutifully checked his order.

"Looks like one of the items had been on back order," she told him. This had delayed the shipment which was shipped just two days earlier.

"The back-ordered item has come in and the package was sent out two days ago," she assured him.

Roger, however, was upset because the original salesperson had promised a quick shipment when he placed the order.

"Well, the salesperson shouldn't have said that," she said. "But there's nothing I can do about that now."

"Did you ship the package by air to make up for the error?" Roger asked.

"No. It went out regular delivery," she answered.

With growing frustration and anger, Roger explained how he had to have the items before the weekend, adding that if the items did not arrive by Friday at noon, he would have to purchase them from a local store. But the service rep was unmoved by his plight.

"Sir, if you don't want the items, you need to return them and we'll credit your charge card for the order and return shipping."

Roger hung up, furious at the customer service rep's attitude. He didn't know whether he would get his merchandise on time or have to do some last minute scrambling to get the equipment he needed. Luckily, the order did arrive the next day, two days before his trip. But his experience with this customer rep expressing no empathy was so unnerving that he never ordered from the catalog again.

The Right Way: A Simple "I'm Sorry"

In contrast to the previous situation, a simple apology and attempt to make things right can make the difference.

Imagine the same scenario. Roger was going on a hiking trip, needed the equipment, and the salesperson reassured him that the equipment was in stock and would arrive in plenty of time. But it didn't. Then, as before, imagine that Roger called the company with his order number and the service rep checked the order and reported the company had shipped the equipment just two days before. And as before, Roger was agitated and told the customer service rep how the sales rep had reassured him about the timely delivery.

But this time, the service rep listened to Roger's story. Instead of dismissing the problem with a stock answer, she said, "I am really sorry. It looks like we got our wires crossed on this end when we told you all the items were in stock. I know how important this shipment is to you having a good trip. Let me give you my name and direct number. If your order doesn't arrive by tomorrow, call me back and I'll have the item re-sent by overnight delivery. All we ask is that you return the original order to us. We'll even cover your shipping costs for sending back the first order, and we'll deduct that from your original charge.

So there's no charge for the second shipment as long as you return the first order within 30 days. Will that be okay with you?"

"Certainly," Roger agreed. He hung up delighted with the service even though the original error by the salesperson was significant. The sincere concern and reassurance from a customer service rep, who gave him her name, was enough to overcome the salesperson's big error. Roger saw her apology as an apology from the entire company for the salesperson's mistake. The result? Roger remained a loyal customer with the company. In fact, he increased his orders in the future. He knew they would provide outstanding service.

A Tale of Two Customer Service Reps

These stories didn't actually happen. But they could have. They demonstrate a real difference in results due to providing the right and wrong kind of service. When you or your company are wrong, if you apologize with sincerity and use active listening to show you truly care and want to help—that's the formula for practicing the "Art" of outstanding customer service.

The three-fold approach we have just discussed will pay off because you understand the fundamental requirements of the art of customer service based on good interpersonal skills. You know how to effectively deal with customers in difficult as well as everyday routine situations, because you know how to listen empathetically, to respond sincerely, and to apologize when necessary to acknowledge when you or your company are wrong—or when your customer is convinced that you are.

Is the Customer Always Right?

Interesting question. Let's say you make it your practice to apologize. Suddenly you are facing a clearly overdemanding or out-of-control customer. What do you do? Management has to set the policy for how to respond to customers. Employees become especially upset when they are required to deal with customers who are clearly out of line. That customer may be operating on the misguided belief that the "customer is always right." Each company has to set its own policy and then has to empower employees to decide on an appropriate approach to such a problem customer, based on these guidelines.

One large company with over 200 customer service representatives encountered a situation in which many customers called to complain on Friday and Saturday evenings. They often used profanity in expressing their dissatisfaction. Many service reps were extremely upset. Some left the company as a result, which showed up as a high turnover rate in the department. After some thought, the company hammered out a response which both satisfied the service representatives and remained true to the company philosophy of providing outstanding service. Customer service representatives were empowered to respond with the following statement to a customer using profanity: "I know you are upset about what happened and I am here to help you. I need to let you know, however, that if you continue to use profanity, I will terminate this call." The positive impact was immediate. For the first time service representatives felt they had an ally in management. They had been listened to and given a sense of control. Customers who had been abusive either cleaned up their language or

31

went elsewhere. Some customers are best shown the door, especially if they are abusive, demeaning, or otherwise out of line.

Each company must decide on an approach to take when dealing with challenging customers. Such an individual decision will address the issue of when and where to draw the line which customers can't cross. This decision needs to reflect the values and corporate culture of each organization, so it will naturally differ from company to company. This is no easy matter, figuring out how to deal with difficult customers. But it is best to have clear company guidelines, so employees know how to respond appropriately. And the implementation of a policy should not be limited to discussions among upper level managers. If you are a front-line employee and have no such "recovery policy" in your department or company, consider the options you have for bringing this topic up with your supervisor or manager. On the other hand, if you are a manager, it might not be a bad idea to ask your front-line staff for examples of how they deal with unruly customers and if they need more support in this area.

Summing Up the Art of Customer Service
One basic truth to remember:

Artistic or emotion-oriented customer service requires interpersonal ability.

And this formula is important to put to use:

Interpersonal ability
= Active/Empathetic Listening
+ Sincerity
+ Apologies When You Are Wrong
* or the Customer Is Convinced*
* You Are*

Put all of these skills together and you have the basics of artful customer service, constructed on courteous, friendly behavior. You will also be able to adapt to the situation using your skills for active/empathetic listening, being sincere, and apologizing when warranted, as you seek to make things right.

Chapter 3

Practicing the "Science" of Customer Service

Setting Priorities The Disney Way

Now we need to look at the other side of the scale, at the "science" of customer service. This science is grounded in providing the correct information the customer needs in an effective way. This information-oriented approach contrasts to the emotion-oriented approach. But it is just as integral to providing high quality service, since both are essential. Or, as the original customer satisfaction equation illustrates, to get customer satisfaction, you need the following:

Excellent product

+ Balance of Art and SCIENCE

= Customer Satisfaction

This side of the service balance is actually easier to learn, compared to the nuances of the art of customer service. It is much easier to master the science basics, since these depend on the hard facts of knowledge. And as a service representative, the fundamentals of knowledge you need to have are:

- Product/Service/Customer Knowledge
- Job/Company Knowledge

You need some basic knowledge in each area just to perform your job. You need a general understanding of the range of products and services your company offers and the rules, policies, and procedures governing job performance. How demanding are your customers? What level of expertise do they expect from you? If you aspire to really outstanding customer service, you have to go beyond the basics. Strive for excellence in these areas. Try to know more than what is expected of you. The greater your depth of information the better, if you balance this knowledge with the "soft" qualities that make up the art or emotional component of excellent service.

How well do you or your employees know your product or service or the job or the company? Think about the following discussion from both the perspective of management or as one of the employees on the front lines dealing with customers.

Product/Service/Customer Knowledge

Excellence in product or service knowledge means you know fully the range of products and services offered by your company or department. This includes knowing about product and service benefits, pricing, the various ways customers can best use these products and services, and how they compare to the competition. You'll end up with the kind of deep understanding of these products and services a salesperson might have. When customers come to you, you fully <u>know</u> their experience of buying or using the product or service.

Look at your company's offerings from the eyes of your customers. Ask yourself some questions. How user-friendly is your website? What happened when you tried to return a faulty or otherwise unwanted product? Do your policies and procedures make life easy for employees, but create headaches for your customers? Alternatively, do your policies and procedures make life easy for your customers but drive good employees away? By looking at what your company does for your customers and knowing what they are likely to expect, you know better how to deal with any problems that can occur when your customers' expectations aren't met. Or when they have unrealistic expectations that they shouldn't have.

Check over the following list of what any employee dealing with customers should know. Gauge your knowledge or an employee's knowledge (if you are a manager) of your company's products and services. Service representatives should have the following type of knowledge. Do you (or your employees) have it?

- The benefits and features offered by your products and services
- The strengths and weaknesses of your company's products or services compared to those offered by competitors

- The pricing of your company's products or services
- How your prices compare with those of competing products or services
- Upcoming changes to your products or services
- The range of uses of your products or services
- Special conditions that affect your products or services, such as special warranties, guarantees, and availability restrictions

When you have in-depth knowledge, you can be extremely helpful to the customer, especially when a customer needs information or help. These are some common ways a service representative can aid a customer. Customers may need help in using a product, guidance in choosing what product or service to use. They may feel dissatisfied because the product hasn't met initial expectations, or may have a complaint about poor product performance.

Think about some situations where this in-depth knowledge can be critical in making a sale or in having a satisfied vs. dissatisfied customer who has already purchased a product.

- The hotel staff knows which rooms are the quietest, so they can direct the guests who want quiet to these rooms.
- The insurance account reps fully understand the latest benefits of their new policies, so they can explain them to both current and new customers.
- The restaurant staff knows how a meal is prepared and which substitutions can be made, so they can satisfy customers who ask for changes in the menu or who have special dietary needs.

• Equipment salespeople can explain how a product's features differ from those offered by the competition and why these differences provide an important benefit for customers.

• A customer rep for a mail order company understands what the company's policy allows, so she can take the initiative and effectively resolve problems on her own in certain situations, such as in the case of a mail order delay, as described earlier.

The more product and policy knowledge an employee has, the better he or she can serve the customer. Having this knowledge may tip the balance in favor of making a sale, retaining an external customer, or maintaining the support of employees or team members, who are the internal customers.

To Know or Not to Know

We all know the difference between having product or service knowledge or not. We've probably all been in the situation of expecting, needing a service representative who was knowledgeable but finding that person may have known even less than we do. Most frustrating. As a service representative, you may have also been on the service end, and been quite unable to provide enough information to satisfy your customer's need. That may have left you feeling like a failure.

The Awful Cost

Let's call him John. He wants a new stereo system for his car. He hops in his car and drives over to the local electronics store. He's all set to buy a new stereo. Once in the store, he's overwhelmed. Not five or ten different models greet him. He's got 40 models to choose from and a confusing array of options.

Puzzled, John is happy when a salesperson comes by.

"Can I help you make your selection?" The salesperson is quiet friendly. A good sign.

"I have a twelve-year-old car," John explains. "I want to figure out what units would work best with my car." He is particularly concerned about whether the unit would fit into his dashboard and if he'll need an antenna.

"Well, I'm not sure about the antenna," the salesperson says. "In fact, I don't usually work in this department. I'm just filling in for Tony. He just went to lunch. He'll be back in about an hour."

"Is there someone else?" John asks.

"I work in home stereos so I don't know much about car systems."

"Maybe I'll stop by another time," John says. Then he leaves the store to read up on car stereos before he comes back. Or find a store with someone who knows something. He is disappointed. He'd been planning on buying the stereo today!

Making the Sale

Poor John! Fortunately for him, that's not the end of the story. Driving back home, John spots another electronics store.

"What the heck. I'll give it another try," he says to himself.

"Can I help you?" Again there is a friendly salesperson offering help.

And again John asks his questions about the best system to buy for his old car. But this salesperson really knows his stuff. He fully understands the different features, benefits, and prices of the different models, and spends about ten minutes giving John a thorough education about the pros and cons of different features and benefits. As a result, John buys the stereo right then, feeling confident and satisfied he has purchased the best system for his needs and budget.

While the above story is an imagined scenario, the same type of thing happens every day. A customer comes in, asks a question. If the salesperson doesn't know the answer and the customer can't find another salesperson who does in a short period of time, the customer will likely go elsewhere. A sale will be lost. By contrast, a knowledgeable salesperson—or one who can quickly respond by grabbing a knowledgeable specialist—can give the customer the information and reassurance he needs to make the purchase. Such knowledge becomes even more critical when a customer has to make a decision about a technically complex or expensive product or service. You need that knowledge to close the sale.

Before placing blame on the salesperson in the first scenario, take into consideration the staffing and training policies of the store. It is up to the store manager or scheduler to understand the strengths and weaknesses of each salesperson when assigning shifts. And it is management's responsibility not to have an inexperienced employee left alone to deal with customers, whether in person, over the telephone, or on the Internet. Not just individual employees need to be responsible for having knowledge. Managers and executives have to know what their employees know, so they can deploy and schedule them properly, and so that the employees doing a particular job will be informed and effective. Another role of management in treating employees as internal customers is to create a trusting environment. In such an environment, it is likely that an employee would feel comfortable telling his manager that he didn't have enough knowledge of the product line to be left alone during a lunch break. He might even request more technical training in the future. On the other hand, if an employee is made to feel foolish or inadequate for asking "stupid" questions or being honest, rest assured that managers will never know the true abilities of their staff members. It is vitally important for managers and employees to collaborate in the development of standard operating procedures as explained below.

Job/Company Knowledge

Beyond knowing about your company's products or services, each employee needs to know the range and limits of the job. This includes knowing the company's policies on such things as the return of merchandise, claims about unsatisfactory service, and whether a customer can pay by check instead of a credit card. The employee needs to know any special industry and legal requirements—if a patient without insurance can pay cash for a doctor's office visit or whether the company can make an adjustment on a returned check charge if a customer has a good excuse. The employee needs to know how much to act independently or when he or she needs to call in a supervisor. Besides knowing how to answer various front-line questions and knowing what decisions are possible in different situations—when to offer credits, discounts, and refunds—it's important to know when to call in the cavalry.

Employees also need to know about the company's overall mission and goals, and perhaps some general background on the company's history, how it was started, and by whom. Why? Well, that way the employee can talk effectively to external customers. In addition, familiarity with the company's traditions and history can help an employee feel part of the corporate culture.

All too often employees aren't well prepared to provide good service. How many times have you started a job with little if any training? How many companies hire new people and then throw them into their jobs and tell them to "just do it" because "there isn't time for training?" These employees are ill equipped to provide good service, let alone aim for outstanding customer service. As a result, many employees don't know how to analyze their customer service approach, much less improve it.

Downsizing! That's another good customer service killer. Many companies have had to dramatically cut down on the number of employees to remain competitive. Those employees left are overloaded with too much responsibility.

The Disney Example

The good news is that good training is possible. And it makes financial sense. The sink or swim approach to new hires stands in stark contrast to the extensive training provided to employees at The Walt Disney Company, where I used to work. Disney is known for its outstanding customer service. Starting with the first day on the job, <u>all</u> employees have to participate in an extensive new-hire orientation program at the Disney University. This program, lasting a full day, exposes all employees to the company's values and history. Obviously this is much more comprehensive than what happens in many companies today, where new hire orientation programs look something like this: "Welcome to the company. Here is your employee handbook. Please sign your non-disclosure agreement. Your department is on floor 23. Oh, and, by the way, good luck." Exaggerated? A little bit, but not that unusual in this day and age.

By contrast, at the Disney University, after new hires finish their day of corporate orientation, they are far from done. Depending on their job and experience, representatives from the company's operating divisions meet them, and they embark on an extensive on-the-job training regimen with close supervision and feedback by an experienced supervisor. As a result of this process, all employees at Disneyland comes to thoroughly understand the company and their respective jobs before ever interacting with a customer.

When I worked at Disney, we boiled our key messages down to make them easy to remember. The company's vision was quite simply expressed as this:

"Create the Happiest Place on Earth"

To achieve that vision, we repeatedly emphasized the following set of priorities, so all employees clearly understood and *lived* them on the job:

#1 = Safety
#2 = Courtesy
#3 = Show
#4 = Capacity

Employees were taught that these four priorities must be followed.

Safety: This was the number one priority for everyone. Park employees were constantly reminded that if they noticed an unsafe situation which could injure an employee or customer, they should immediately stop doing their job (as long as this wasn't dangerous) and fix whatever was unsafe (such as moving an object that could trip a customer or employee), or call for assistance.

Courtesy: Once safety was assured, the employee's second priority was to be courteous and friendly to customers. This meant more than just being polite. To be courteous, employees were told to go the extra mile to help, such as guiding a lost customer to the restaurant he or she couldn't find. They were also taught to make their gestures more courteous, such as pointing with an open hand, instead of a single finger, when directing customers on to the rides. Plus being courteous meant smiling and having a good time!

Show: The third priority was the concept of "show," which meant keeping everything clean and well maintained—from the clothes the employees wore to the rides and even the bathrooms. Even though a full staff of custodial employees worked to keep the park clean, all employees were encouraged to be on the lookout for areas of the park that were "bad show" and to either take care of the problem themselves or to call for help. Whether it was a wet seat on a boat, wads of gum stuck on a chair, or dirty windows, we all kept an eye out to maintain the show. The goal was to have the entire park sparkling clean. The notion of keeping it spic and span was impressed on all employees, whatever their jobs.

Capacity: Once the other priorities were met, the last priority was really more of an expectation that the number of customers who came to the park each day would take care of itself. Though management kept careful observations of the attendance and capacity of each attraction and restaurant on an hourly basis, the philosophy was that if you took care of the <u>Safety</u> of the employees and customers, were <u>Courteous</u> to each other, and maintained the <u>Show</u>, the customers would show up and capacity would take care of itself. The goal was satisfied and *loyal* customers who kept returning.

In addition to this emphasis on serving customers, the company also stressed that all employees were the members of a team or family, which was carrying out the company's vision. No single person was more important than others in providing outstanding customer service. This is what we told the new employees at the end of the orientation program before they could even set foot in the park and interact with the customers, or "Guests" as Disney called them:

The Walt Disney Company has spent millions of dollars over the years to create and maintain Disneyland as "The Happiest Place On Earth" using a number of approaches. These include:
Paying great attention to even the smallest details,
Setting extremely high standards, communicating them clearly, and expecting everyone to meet them,
Investing in the proper training of all employees before they

encounter the Guests, so they know how to act and what to say.

You have to view Disneyland as a finely-tuned environment geared toward the complete satisfaction of the Guests. Consider all areas of the park which the Guest sees and enjoys as a "stage," and remember when "on stage," you must "act out your roles" in an appropriate manner. That's why we call the people who work at Disneyland" Cast Members," and not employees. Our Guests come to Disneyland to escape the worries and harshness of the outside world, and it is up to you, the Cast Members, to help make their dreams come true.

Unfortunately, one harsh word or inappropriate body language by a Cast Member can undermine the work of the whole team. For example, say a family comes to Disneyland and spends the whole day enjoying the attractions, food, and environment. They leave after the fireworks feeling completely happy. But then, as they drive out of the parking lot and the driver is confused about which exit to use to get to the highway, the driver asks a Cast Member in the parking lot for directions. Sure, the Cast Member may feel harried by trying to control the thousands of cars heading toward the exit. But if he barks back: "Look, just keep moving, you can read the signs when you get out on the street," and brusquely waves the car on, the driver is likely to feel angry and dismissed. As a result, in a split second, the Cast Member could very well undermine the previous ten hours of great joy the family experienced. Then, in that instant, the memories of all of the friendly Cast Members, the cleanliness, and the glitter and beauty of Disneyland could be replaced with a final memory of anger and disgust.

As this story illustrates, positive customer interaction is crucial for continued success. A negative interaction can undermine a huge investment in a beautiful, comfortable environment. Think about your own company—how much money and time you have invested in your product or service, in advertising to attract customers, and in your company's facilities. Too many companies devote most of their budget to the tangible "hardware" of the business. They invest in their products and in their plant and facilities, from creating glitzy showrooms to showplace resorts. But these companies often fail to ensure their success with the key components necessary for this in the form of knowledgeable, courteous, friendly, and helpful employees. But such employees are absolutely part of the essential bottom line—as underlined throughout this book.

A Note About Empowerment

Employees most assuredly need in-depth knowledge about the company's products and services and their job. But there's still more. They need to be empowered to make decisions. These components for success—empowerment plus knowledge—go hand in hand. Ironically, many companies discuss the value of expanding *power* to those on the front lines. However, if employees are to effectively exercise this power, they need the *knowledge* to go with it when they interact with customers. They need to make informed decisions, and to have this knowledge they must be fully trained on product or service information and on company policy and job requirements and limitations. This way, and only this way, can they make solid decisions based on knowledge.

To fully empower employees, management must provide them with the appropriate training, which includes not only the knowledge, but decision-making skills. This way, they will know how to apply this information and truly feel empowered by it.

Some companies give only lip service to the concept of "empowerment," so it becomes more like an empty management buzzword of the day than a real transfer of power. As if just saying this word and telling employees "you're empowered" meant anything. These managers and executives pat themselves on the back for empowering employees because they said the right words. But if management doesn't back up that message of empowerment with the tools of empowerment, which require having both knowledge and management support for decision-making, frontline employees won't feel empowered and won't act that way. It's imperative—those in management have to provide employees with the proper training, guidance, and support for them to feel and act truly empowered. If not, they will simply feel confused, isolated, and responsible, and won't be able to use the knowledge they have for effective decision making.

This is the essence—employees need to have both the know-how (knowledge) to apply the science of customer service, along with management backing to make decisions effectively. With that in their back pocket, they can take this science of customer service and add the interpersonal skills that make up the art of customer service to achieve a balanced approach. The winning combination is when they mix that balance with product quality. The result is customer satisfaction—the ultimate goal of the customer service professional.

Here's another equation to remember. The knowledge that forms the scientific/information part of the customer service looks something like :

Scientific or information-oriented customer service

= Technical Ability

Technical ability

= Product/Service/Customer Knowledge

+ Job Knowledge

+ Company Knowledge

Let's look back at our balance equation and think about the end result.

A Balance of Science and Art

+ a Quality Product

= Outstanding Service

= CUSTOMER SATISFACTION

Your Ultimate Customer Service Goal

Chapter 4

Assessing the "Culture" of Your Organization

Companies seem to have a sort of personality. Often we call this the organizational culture. A company or specific units in this company tend to lean more one direction than the other. Some are more scientific/rational; others more art/emotion oriented. For example, certain professions that are more technical or bottom line-oriented—think about engineering firms, R&D departments, legal departments, manufacturing divisions, computer companies, and agricultural suppliers—tend to have a more scientific, technical, no-nonsense approach. By contrast, professions that are more service oriented—let's say human resource departments, sales departments, retailers, nurses, and customer service divisions—are more artistic/emotion-oriented. These different types of companies generally continue to use their different approaches, since the approach has worked for them, and their employees and customers have grown to accept and expect it.

This may be like the old "if it isn't broke, don't fix it." Truth is, the way to an even healthier bottom line and more customer and employee satisfaction, is through a balance of both sides. The one sided approach—no matter which direction a company goes in—doesn't work *as well* as the balanced approach with both the art and science integrated.

Assess Your Employees' Skills to Achieve Balance

There's more than one way to achieve balance. If you are a manager you can try for a balance with a mix of employees who can offer the two orientations. Sometimes this is achieved by pairing science-oriented employees with art-oriented employees. In the ideal situation, some people have the ability to combine these approaches and can apply *either*, depending on the needs and demands of their customers. Or if employees don't initially have these skills in sufficient measure, you as a manager can develop these skills in them through awareness and skills training.

Start here. Figure out where you stand now. As a manager, look at your team. Assess the skills of all the members of your team. Learn who can do what in serving your customers. As you do this assessment, think of how different employees can fit different needs and what skills might be lacking or may be developed.

As you go through this process, you're likely to find some people at the extremes, while others have more of a mix of traits. You may have people on the team who seem to be highly gifted with "scientific" or technical knowledge and reasoning ability, although these folks may lack people skills. Often they lack these good people abilities because they have learned to work alone. Or they staff a unit of the company where people skills don't matter as much since they are evaluated on technical competence. Your tendency might be to keep them far away from interacting with customers. You may fear they will be insensitive and insult others with their frankness and offhand remarks. For example, if such a person encounters a customer having trouble understanding a technical product, he might readily show his frustration by getting irritated, walking away, or even telling the customer he is too dense to understand. Obviously such behavior is crude and off-putting. Don't despair. There may still be hope. Perhaps you can help this person round off his rough edges and become more balanced through learning some basic people skills. Maybe one-on-one coaching and training will help. Or team this person up with others with more people skills to act as role models. Maybe the person's knowledge is invaluable to the team or company. You may want to insulate him from negatively impacting co-workers or external customers by finding him a place to work in a back office. But if there isn't time, money, or patience enough, it may be best to let the high-knowledge but poor-in-people-skills person go.

But let's look at the other side of this continuum. You will find people who are truly nice, highly attentive, and sensitive. They know just what to say and how to say it to create good rapport with a customer or other employee. They are whizzes at interacting with and understanding others. However, they are not perfect. They often cannot answer technical questions because they don't have the in-depth product and technical knowledge. Why not? It may be that they lack an interest in technical matters, so they never learn or when they do, they promptly forget. Some of these "people people" consider learning detailed knowledge a distraction from what they consider their real job—

interacting with customers in a supportive way. Whatever their reason for not knowing, they are only effective on the "artistic" or emotional side of customer service. While they are making nice with customers, they are letting them down by not having the kinds of information customers want. Now, customers may appreciate their personal warmth, but if the customers' need for information and technical knowledge goes unfilled, they may go elsewhere.

The bottom line is this—if you or your staff interact with customers in an unbalanced manner, whether by being too technical and science-oriented or too emotional and art-oriented, you risk losing customers and sales. Not only that, this unbalanced approach can lose you employees, or prevent you from getting ones that contribute to the balance you need for success.

Think about it. If you have a lopsided company culture, you're going to lose out because you'll attract and keep employees on the side of the balance scale you already have. That's because they will feel more comfortable in that setting. And your company or team becomes even more unbalanced. That state of imbalance will continue unless you act to shift the weight of your company's cultural tradition, by seeking out a different type of employee to help you swing back into balance.

Look at the Carmakers

Don't just take my word for it. Look at some important points in our business/economic history. Think of the problems of the American automotive industry. For so long the king, this industry experienced a severe and well-deserved decline in the 1980s because the Big Three (General Mo-

tors, Ford, Chrysler) failed in two key areas:
- They didn't listen to their customers, so they weren't practicing "Art" of customer service.
- They didn't provide high quality, reliable products, as compared to their competition, so they weren't practicing the "Science" of customer service either.

The sum total for neglect in these two areas resulted in well-publicized loss of billions of dollars in sales and the tremendous erosion of market share for the Big Three. This is when foreign competitors stepped in with more reliable, higher-quality cars and with a greater responsiveness to the customer's demand for better service.

Faced with prospects of a further decline in profits and market share, the Big Three fought back with a big push to improve quality and provide products the consumer wanted. The result? The three U.S. companies once again experienced increased profits and market share. They approached their strategizing in a rational, scientific way. But they combined the science of producing good products with listening to their customers' emotional needs. Then, they artfully met those needs with the products their customers demanded.

Their problems were not over yet. Despite of the manufacturers' more balanced efforts, many consumers resisted going to the dealerships to purchase automobiles because they hated facing "the pushy sales people." They didn't like high-pressure sales tactics or the sales staffers who insulted female customers by ignoring them or acting in a condescending manner. Some customers were fed up with service people who treated them with a lack of respect, claiming they were wrong when they complained of poor car performance. The lack of balance at the dealership service level hurt the car manufacturers as well. Fewer cars were sold.

The industry listened one more time. Many dealers adopted a one-price, "no haggle" approach to sales. The Saturn Corporation, a General Motors subsidiary, pioneered this. Training came first. The dealers invested in customer service training for their sales and service employees to make sure all employees treated all with customer respect. Salespeople were trained to sell in a different way, without pressure tactics. Service area employees were trained to actively listen to customers so they could quickly pinpoint the source of a car's problem on the first visit. This meant customers wouldn't have to return several times before the problem was discovered.

Backed by an advertising and promotional campaign to create customer awareness, this new approach eventually paid off. By the early 1990s, the Big Three enjoyed increased sales. Their customers now knew the dealers were selling good, reliable products and their service people could not only help maintain these cars but would make the customers feel appreciated. This effort to improve quality and service was so successful that one of the Big Three, General Motors, began selling its Saturn cars in Japan in numbers that no other U.S. automaker had ever approached!

Service started to become a competitive factor. Manufacturers and dealers could no longer rely primarily or solely on great quality, reliability, or a competitive price to beat other car manufacturers. Now they needed sales people with both a high level of interpersonal skill and of technical knowledge to appeal to customers. And their service people had to get the job done right the first time. They had to tell customers clearly what needed fixing without making them feel "stupid." In short, the car industry's successful turnaround after a period of declining sales showed the Big Three that the dealers had to back up the manufacturer with both the *science* and the *art* of customer service, which customers now demanded.

Don't Follow This Example

Some people don't quite get it. Here's one example of what can go wrong when you don't approach customers with the proper balance.

Since we've been talking about the automobile industry, let's stick with cars. Let's visit a showroom with a family.

They'd had three children, so the young couple was ready for a car that would fit this family. It needed to be a sort of family bus as well as fit the bill for car pooling. A minivan was ideal, they decided. Just what they needed. Researching the available models, they decided on a make and model that would best meet their needs.

Good shoppers, they visited six dealerships that sold the model and got a price on the model they wanted. They also interviewed the service departments at each dealer to compare their services and hours of operation. Especially important was finding a service department that was open on weekends, since they wanted the option to have their van serviced then as well as during the week.

With all the research completed, they made a decision. Price won out. And, fortunately for them, this dealership had the friendliest, most knowledgeable sales staff and a superior service department.

"We'll take it," they told the salesman when they came back to their chosen dealer. When they began writing up the paperwork with the salesman, everything went fine until they went to the finance department thinking they just had to finish the paperwork to obtain the financing and close the sale.

"You need stain treatment for your upholstery," the finance manager insisted.

"No," they told him. "It's fine the way it is."

"You have to have a car alarm system. You don't want the car stolen," the finance manager insisted.

"We really aren't interested in any extras," the couple replied. They knew what they wanted and their bottom line. "We'll just take the car for the price we agreed upon."

"You're a smart couple. I can't believe you wouldn't want to protect your investment. You'll want rust proofing as well. Let me show you what that will come to when you add—"

"We'll take it as is."

He continued in his sales pitch.

The couple not only refused again, but they were so angry that the finance manager seemed to care only about making the additional sale that they stormed out of his office. Then, they headed to a dealer across town that offered the same car and made their purchase there—at a higher price!

The owner of the dealership had spent thousands of dollars to train the sales and service staff in both technical and interpersonal service techniques, but he didn't train everyone. He left out the finance department, and lost a sale as a result. Thinking only of his check, the finance manager thought he could make an extra commission by pushing a few extra products, and he knew them well. But while he had the science of his products down pat, his art of being responsive to his customer's needs and wants was sorely lacking. Thus, he tore down everything the others in the company were trying to build up, and he lost both the sale of the automobile and a future customer for the service portion of the dealership.

Another Unbalanced Situation

But a lack of balance in the other direction of knowing the art of customer service without the underlying science can be just as destructive. That's what happened in the following situation.

When she went shopping for new furniture, Ruth decided to hire an interior designer. "It'll save me time," she told herself. She responded to an ad in the local paper and hit it off right way with Helen, the designer. Helen was warm and personable, as she showed Ruth several unique color combinations for fabrics that Ruth decided would work well in her living room. Talking about interior design trends, the two women laughed and talked like old friends. This was a good combination! Finally, Helen helped Ruth select an expensive, elegant sofa and contrasting chairs. They topped it off with a glass top coffee table.

Ruth was delighted with the purchase for the first two months. Soon her pleasant feelings began to fade as the pale, silk-blend fabric on the sofa, which Helen had recommended, also began to fade. On top of that, the sofa picked up noticeable stains from the slightest causes, such as the oil from a hand on the armrest, while the glass top coffee table in front of the sofa instantly registered the slightest fingerprint or coffee stain. Ruth had three young children and a cat . (The latter soon put tears in the fabric.) One thing Helen had neglected to do was to ask Ruth about her living situation. Her recommendation didn't take into account the hard wear the furniture would be getting.

Ruth's delight soon turned to chagrin for making the purchase, especially when she had the added expense of reupholstering the sofa with a more practical fabric and replacing the coffee table with one that didn't show the dirt immediately and need constant cleaning.

Ruth complained. Helen simply made the excuse, "You didn't tell me about your pets and children, so how was I supposed to know?"

Truth is, it was Helen's job, as the designer, to know what to ask. It wasn't up to the client to ask the right questions about fabric durability. That's why Ruth hired a designer. She was an expert. She was hired for her knowledge. A knowledgeable designer would inquire about lifestyle issues and recommend appropriate product lines.

While Helen might have gained the first sale from Ruth due to her personality and their good rapport, she lost any future sales, because she didn't balance the art of customer service with the science of product knowledge.

The Right Balance Can Make the Sale

While a lack of balance in the *art* and *science* can result in problems, knowing how to shift the balance, as needed, can make the sale. That's what happened in the following case.

Sally needed a digital camera. She was going to put pictures in computer-based presentations and on her Web site.

Top of the line, she decided, was what she would buy. She got a quote of $900 plus a 20% service override on a name-brand camera from her computer consultant who had set up and continued to upgrade her system.

Sally was a little reticent. She didn't know much about this recommended camera, other than its name. And another thing bothered her—should she get a camera from her computer expert? What if she needed some camera repairs or had questions on how to use it? And frankly, the consultant didn't know much technical information about the camera—she just knew it had excellent resolution.

Sally headed off to her local camera shop, only a mile away. Better to purchase the camera there, she decided, as long as the price was close to the price her consultant had quoted. Better to let her computer consultant focus on computers. She parked across the street from the shop at a meter with six minutes left. "I can just run in quickly and get some sale sheets and a quote on the camera I want," she told herself. She didn't have any quarters in her pockets.

Sally went inside and spoke briefly to a salesman who was waiting on a man who was looking at the recommended camera and another high-end model.

"No, I don't have any sale sheets," he told Sally.

His other customer left so Sally quickly told him what she wanted. "I want the best resolution I can get," she told him. "I'm using this for my website and for presentations."

"I'm not sure you really want that camera," the salesman told her. "I think you'd be just as satisfied with a model that doesn't have as high a resolution. After all, you're only talking about Internet or presentation graphics. You can get by with less."

He then he pulled out several cameras, reeling off details about their technical merits and showing obvious pride in his knowledge.

As he rattled on, Sally worried about her expiring meter. It would be rude to walk away while the salesman was pulling out the cameras and looking in his book to give her price quotes, she thought. Besides, she wanted a quote on the camera she originally asked about.

She sighed, hoping her impatience was obvious. The salesman had to flip through several pages to find the quotes for the two high-end cameras she found of interest and the other three lower-cost cameras he had picked out as more suitable for her purpose. The salesperson was blind to her body language and didn't notice her tone of voice. She was impatient because she wasn't interested in the lower-priced cameras. But the sales person continued on, trying to convince her that she didn't need such an expensive camera.

He admitted in the end that perhaps if Sally later wanted to do more professional work with prints, the better cameras would be more appropriate.

Finally the salesman gave her the information she originally requested. Sally ran out of the store with his card, on which he had written several price quotes, but she was annoyed. She felt disrespected, almost insulted. The salesman tried to steer her from the high-end camera to a lower priced one—only a few hundred dollars less anyway. He clearly had not taken time to fully understand her desire to get the best model. And his attitude was condescending. He made her feel like she didn't deserve a better camera, since she didn't have much technical knowledge about it.

When Sally got to her car, she noticed the paper under her windshield wiper. She had gotten a parking ticket! The extra few minutes the salesperson kept her while talking about cameras that didn't interest her were enough for the meter to expire, and just enough time to get a ticket.

That camera shop was out, Sally decided. Then, to Sally's surprise, her computer consultant, who didn't know much about cameras to start with, had researched the digital camera market and found out just the information she needed. The consultant then combined her new knowledge with her sensitivity to Sally's needs to provide Sally with just the kind of service and support she wanted. Sally compared the store price with her consultant's estimate, and saw her cost would be only about $100 more. She decided to buy the camera from her consultant. Sally was willing to spend the extra money, because the consultant had been so responsive in finding out about the kind of camera she said she wanted and hadn't tried to sell her on something she didn't want. It would also save Sally any extra time she would have had to spend to finish comparing the features of the cameras she saw at the store.

While the camera store salesman had lots of knowledge, his lack of artfulness blew the sale. The computer consultant acquired the necessary knowledge and combined that with her customer awareness. She not only continued to upgrade Sally's computer, but she made the camera sale too.

The Customer Service Balancing Act Questionnaire

Knowing how to create a balanced customer service approach can make a big difference in customer satisfaction. In order to change how you interact with your customers or with your employees (as a supervisor or manager), the first step is to assess where you or your employees currently stand in each of the art and science areas. On the following pages there is an assessment tool to help determine how you and others in your company stack up in achieving this art-science balance.

This can be done individually and in teams. The benefit of involving teams of people is that you can get a more well-rounded assessment of many areas of the department, company, or operation. It can also stimulate robust discussions that result in not only better service to your external customers, but lead to better teamwork within and between departments. However, the assessment can be less than beneficial if staff members feel uncomfortable sharing openly with each other or the boss. If that's the case, consider having a professional business consultant, unknown to your staff, do the assessment after experiencing your service as an anonymous customer or mystery shopper. You may also want to ask your customers if they would like to participate in a survey. In this case, a focus group would work. You'll need to modify the questions slightly to ensure the items in the questionnaire are areas customers could observe and comment on. Then, you can go over the assessment with them. Try offering them a lunch and free product or other gesture of thanks for their time and honest opinion.

The survey form begins on page 69. Feel free to make a copy (or copies), so you or whoever is responding to the survey can fill in the answers.

Using the Customer Service Balancing Act Questionnaire

The following questionnaire will show how well balanced you and/or your organization are in providing outstanding customer service.

To recap the basic ideas presented in this chapter, you want a balance in the "Art" and "Science" areas of service, because being out of balance increases your odds of creating *the pain of neglect* for customers. Being in balance increases the ways you create the *joy of attention*. Use this questionnaire to find your areas of strength, so you can maximize them. Or this will help to identify your weaknesses, so you can improve in these areas and reduce the greater odds of lost customers and lost sales.

The questionnaire is for you, your staff, or your customers to fill out. Again, you can develop different questions for internal staff and external customers. Copy the whole questionnaire to answer all the questions or tell respondents which questions to answer. Or you can choose the questions more appropriate for your situation and copy them to create a customized questionnaire. Feel free to rewrite any questions to better suit your own situation.

The Balance of Art and Science Used in Designing the Questionnaire

The questions are designed to explore how well either you or your team does in each of the elements comprising the balance of art and science. As previously discussed, the art and science of customer service is composed of these elements shown on the next page.

ART	SCIENCE
• Emotion	• Technical Knowledge
• Attitudes	• Skills
• Intuition	• Research Findings
• Heart	• Sufficient Quantity of Product
• Quality of Interaction	• Knowledge of Systems and Policies

EXCELLENT PRODUCT

Remember:

Excellent product

+ Balance of Art and Science

= Joy of Attention

and Customer Satisfaction

Excellent Product

+ No Balance of Art and Science

= Pain of Neglect and

Customer Dissatisfaction

Poor or Unsatisfactory Product

+/or No Balance of Art and Science

= Pain of Neglect and Customer

Dissatisfaction

The survey builds on the following "Art" and "Science" divisions and subcategories, using questions in each area to assess how well balanced you or your team are in that area. More specifically, the questions cover these key areas shown on the next page.

Categories of Questions on the Customer Service Questionnaire

Art	Science
Quality of Delivery	Quality of Product
Product or Service Knowledge	Product or Service Knowledge
Working Environment	Working Environment
Working Conditions: Teamwork	Working Conditions: Equipment
Policies and Standards	Policies and Standards
Problem Solving: Support	Problem Solving: Knowledge
Customer Support: Appreciation	Customer Support: Actions
Training: Interpersonal / Cultural	Training: Technical / Policy
Quality Performance: Effectiveness	Quantity Performance: Efficiency

The Customer Service Questionnaire: How's Your Balance?

The following questions will help you assess your own or your employees' customer service balance. The first set of questions deals with the science of customer service; the second set deals with the art of providing this service. The final questions will help you assess how well you are doing in these areas and where to improve. Afterwards, you can use the chart and instruction guide to help you analyze the questionnaire results individually or for your whole team or company.

To answer the questions, circle the appropriate number. Be specific when writing your comments.

I. Your Balance of Science and Art: Measuring your product or service and how you deliver it.

The Science of Customer Service Total Science Score:____

Quality of Product

1. The product or service that my company, division, or team delivers where I am working is of high quality.

Disagree		Neutral		Agree	Don't
1	2	3	4	5	Know

Comments: _____

_____

_____

_____

2. The product or service my company, division, or team delivers is constantly reviewed to ensure it has not deteriorated relative to the competition or customers' demands.

Disagree		Neutral		Agree	Don't
1	2	3	4	5	Know

Comments: _____

_____

_____

_____

Product or Service Knowledge

3. Employees in this organization or department can answer almost all questions the customers have about the products or services supported by this department.

Disagree		Neutral		Agree	Don't
1	2	3	4	5	Know

Comments: _____

_____

_____

_____

4. Systems are in place to quickly update employees on changes in the product or service they provide.

Disagree		Neutral		Agree	Don't
1	2	3	4	5	Know

Comments: _____

_____

_____

_____

Working Environment

5. My department/store/factory/facility is normally kept very clean.

Disagree		Neutral		Agree	Don't
1	2	3	4	5	Know

Comments: _____

_____

_____

_____

6. My department/store/factory/facility is safe for both customers and employees.

Disagree		Neutral		Agree	Don't
1	2	3	4	5	Know

Comments: _____

_____

_____

_____

Working Conditions: Equipment

7. My organization uses the most up-to-date equipment, so employees can do their jobs as efficiently and effectively as possible.

Disagree		Neutral		Agree	Don't
1	2	3	4	5	Know

Comments: _____

_____

_____

_____

8. My organization uses the most up-to-date equipment to fulfill customer needs, resulting in high customer satisfaction.

Disagree		Neutral		Agree	Don't
1	2	3	4	5	Know

Comments: _____

_____

_____

_____

Policies and Standards

9. The policies and standards of my company or division take into account the diverse nature of our customers and employees, by recognizing other religious holidays, religious practices, and other differences.

Disagree		Neutral		Agree	Don't
1	2	3	4	5	Know

Comments: _____

_____

_____

_____

10. The policies and standards of my company or division are assessed on a regular basis to ensure they are up to date.

Disagree		Neutral		Agree	Don't
1	2	3	4	5	Know

Comments: _____

_____

_____

_____

Problem Solving: Knowledge

11. All employees in the company or division know exactly what to do (including knowing the limits of what they can do) in almost every problem situation which is likely to occur.

Disagree		Neutral		Agree	Don't
1	2	3	4	5	Know

Comments: _____

_____

_____

_____

12. Employees have the ability to quickly get to the bottom of an issue and solve it.

Disagree		Neutral		Agree	Don't
1	2	3	4	5	Know

Comments: _____

_____

_____

_____

13.   Employees in a division or on a team share information on the source of and solution to problems with each other, so they can better solve these or related problems in the future.

Disagree		Neutral		Agree	Don't
1	2	3	4	5	Know

Comments: _____

_____

_____

_____

14.   In order to leverage knowledge and help others better anticipate and solve similar problems in the future, employees of one division or team share with other divisions and teams the source of and solution to customer problems they have faced.

Disagree		Neutral		Agree	Don't
1	2	3	4	5	Know

Comments: _____

_____

_____

_____

Customer Support: Actions

15.   When customers call with problems or complaints, employees don't send them on a "wild goose chase" by referring them to other departments or sources of information. Instead, employees help customers find the answers themselves.

Disagree		Neutral		Agree	Don't
1	2	3	4	5	Know

Comments: _____

_____

_____

_____

16.   Employees take the initiative to get back to customers as promised, even when they can only indicate they are still working on the issue or are calling to convey "bad news."

Disagree		Neutral		Agree	Don't
1	2	3	4	5	Know

Comments: _____

_____

_____

_____

<u>Training: Technical/Policy</u>

17.   Employees in the company or division receive technical product training, so they better know the answers to problems and can better help to solve the customer's problems.

Disagree		Neutral		Agree	Don't
1	2	3	4	5	Know

Comments: _____

_____

_____

_____

18.   Employees in the company or division receive policy training so they know the answers to problems and can take the initiative in helping solve them.

Disagree		Neutral		Agree	Don't
1	2	3	4	5	Know

Comments: _____

_____

_____

_____

Quantity Performance: Efficiency

19.   Our systems, equipment, or facility layout allow us to handle a varying number of customers, or respond to changing product demands efficiently.

Disagree		Neutral		Agree	Don't
1	2	3	4	5	Know

Comments: _____

_____

_____

_____

20.   Our staffing strategy is flexible, so we can adjust the number of personnel based on the number of customers or on changing product demands.

Disagree		Neutral		Agree	Don't
1	2	3	4	5	Know

Comments: _____

_____

_____

_____

21. We generally have enough products on hand to supply all of our customers.

Disagree		Neutral		Agree	Don't
1	2	3	4	5	Know

Comments: _____

_____

_____

22. We generally have enough service providers on hand to provide support for all of our customers.

Disagree		Neutral		Agree	Don't
1	2	3	4	5	Know

Comments: _____

_____

_____

_____

23.   Our product or service is delivered on time.

Disagree		Neutral		Agree	Don't
1	2	3	4	5	Know

Comments: _____

_____

_____

24. Managers in the company are aware of the unique demands of our customers and the skill levels of employees. As a result, the staffing plan assures that: A) Only fully qualified employees interact with customers or, B) Employees "in training" are paired with skilled employees/mentors.

Disagree		Neutral		Agree	Don't
1	2	3	4	5	Know

Comments: _____

_____

_____

_____

25. Employees are recognized and rewarded for meeting or exceeding business goals.

Disagree		Neutral		Agree	Don't
1	2	3	4	5	Know

Comments: _____

_____

_____

_____

The Art of Customer Service   Total Art Score: _____

Quality of Delivery

1. My group or I deliver our product or service in a pleasant manner to our customers (such as with a smile or positive tone of voice, and using the customer's name).

Disagree		Neutral		Agree	Don't
1	2	3	4	5	Know

Comments: _____

_____

_____

_____

2. My staff or I don't rush customers.

Disagree		Neutral		Agree	Don't
1	2	3	4	5	Know

Comments: _____

_____

_____

_____

Product or Service Knowledge

3. The employees in my organization seek answers to the questions they can't immediately answer.

Disagree		Neutral		Agree	Don't
1	2	3	4	5	Know

Comments: _____

_____

_____

_____

4. The management in my organization creates an environment that encourages employees to seek answers to the questions they can't immediately answer.

Disagree		Neutral		Agree	Don't
1	2	3	4	5	Know

Comments: _____

_____

_____

_____

Working Environment

5. My department, store, or location has a pleasant, customer-centered atmosphere (such as having music, colorful pictures, a comfortable waiting area, or a play area for children).

Disagree		Neutral		Agree	Don't
1	2	3	4	5	Know

Comments: _____

_____

_____

_____

6. My department, store, website, or location is easy for customers to find.

Disagree		Neutral		Agree	Don't
1	2	3	4	5	Know

Comments: _____

_____

_____

_____

Working Conditions: Teamwork

7. My organization fosters a spirit of teamwork, where we work together as a team and help each other out.

Disagree		Neutral		Agree	Don't
1	2	3	4	5	Know

Comments: _____

_____

_____

_____

8. The management of this organization spends time on the "front line" interacting with customers, as well as with the employees who interact regularly with customers.

Disagree		Neutral		Agree	Don't
1	2	3	4	5	Know

Comments: _____

_____

_____

_____

Policies and Standards

9. Signs, policies, instructions, directions, menus, and other printed materials of the organization are written in various languages to reflect the native languages of our employees and customers.

Disagree		Neutral		Agree	Don't
1	2	3	4	5	Know

Comments: _____

_____

_____

_____

10. Policies and procedures are designed with the customer in mind and are user friendly.

Disagree		Neutral		Agree	Don't
1	2	3	4	5	Know

Comments: _____

_____

_____

_____

Problem Solving: Support

11.   Our company has an easy-to-follow resolution process for customers.

Disagree		Neutral		Agree	Don't
1	2	3	4	5	Know

Comments: _____

_____

_____

_____

12.   Our company or division encourages customers to give us feedback about the service they have received and how they feel about it.

Disagree		Neutral		Agree	Don't
1	2	3	4	5	Know

Comments: _____

_____

_____

_____

13. When a customer service problem arises, employees do not make customers feel in the "wrong," by doing thinks like demanding to see receipts. Instead, employees try to make the customer feel "right" by being understanding and apologizing for the inconvenience.

Disagree		Neutral		Agree	Don't
1	2	3	4	5	Know

Comments: _____

_____

_____

_____

14. When problems or misunderstandings arise between departments, (such as between sales and operations), managers and employees commonly use a constructive, collaborative process to discuss the problem and resolve it rather than assigning blame and creating inter-departmental friction.

Disagree		Neutral		Agree	Don't
1	2	3	4	5	Know

Comments: _____

_____

_____

_____

Customer Support: Acknowledgment and Appreciation

15. When dealing with an upset customer, employees commonly acknowledge the customer's feelings of frustration with phrases such as: "I know you have been waiting for a long time and I want to help."

Disagree		Neutral		Agree	Don't
1	2	3	4	5	Know

Comments: _____

_____

_____

_____

16. Employees thank customers who point out service or product shortcomings.

Disagree		Neutral		Agree	Don't
1	2	3	4	5	Know

Comments: _____

_____

_____

_____

Training: Interpersonal / Cultural

17. Employees receive communications training so they can put themselves in the customer's shoes to better understand their customer's concerns and problems.

Disagree		Neutral		Agree	Don't
1	2	3	4	5	Know

Comments: _____

_____

_____

_____

18. Employees receive cross-cultural and/or interpersonal skills training, so they can more effectively relate to and understand the feelings of domestic and foreign-born customers, in addition to dealing with any of their complaints about products or services.

Disagree		Neutral		Agree	Don't
1	2	3	4	5	Know

Comments: _____

_____

_____

_____

Quality Performance: Effectiveness

19. Our <u>software</u> systems allow us to handle a varying number of customers or changing product demands with a high level of customer comfort and convenience.

Disagree		Neutral		Agree	Don't
1	2	3	4	5	Know

Comments: _____

_____

_____

_____

20. Our <u>hardware</u> systems allow us to handle a varying number of customers or changing product demands with a high level of customer comfort and convenience.

Disagree		Neutral		Agree	Don't
1	2	3	4	5	Know

Comments: _____

_____

_____

_____

21. Our facility layout allows us to handle a varying number of customers or changing product demands with a high level of customer comfort and convenience.

Disagree		Neutral		Agree	Don't
1	2	3	4	5	Know

Comments: _____

_____

_____

_____

22. Our staff is rewarded for maintaining a high level of quantity without sacrificing the quality of interaction with the customer.

Disagree		Neutral		Agree	Don't
1	2	3	4	5	Know

Comments: _____

_____

_____

_____

23. Managers of the company are aware of the number of customers and level of demands on front-line employees, so they hire staff with the right blend of Art and Science to handle these customers.

Disagree		Neutral		Agree	Don't
1	2	3	4	5	Know

Comments: _____

_____

_____

_____

24. Managers of the company are aware of the number of customers and level of demands on front-line employees, so they regularly coach employees on how to maintain a high quality of interaction.

Disagree		Neutral		Agree	Don't
1	2	3	4	5	Know

Comments: _____

_____

_____

_____

25. The management team reinforces the importance of maintaining quality interactions with customers and employees alike by participating in educational seminars themselves (such as customer service and leadership skills training).

Disagree		Neutral		Agree	Don't
1	2	3	4	5	Know

Comments: _____

_____

_____

_____

Analyzing the Questionnaire Results

Please remember this is not intended to be a validated, scientific survey instrument. The intention is that this will be a simple model that you can customize for your own business environment to begin the process of identifying your strengths and improvement areas. Some organizations make this type of activity much too complicated and get caught up in the need to create a perfect assessment questionnaire. Some companies are possibly intimidated by the thought of conducting a survey because of the time and expense involved, possibly because all too often the result is inactivity and no one benefits. The key is a device that is simple and delivers information any organization, large or small, can act on. So, look at this questionnaire as a starting point. From here you can begin creating your own approach to continuously assessing your balance.

There are a number of ways to analyze the data that comes from this kind of questionnaire. Depending upon the size and structure of an organization, the results can be analyzed on an individual basis or for a team, department, or the company as a whole. To see how you stack up, tally up the 25 responses found in each of the two sections of this questionnaire, the Science section, then the Art section. Another option, which will yield more detail, is to find the score for each of the nine categories of questions found in each section, then compare them. Use the tally sheets on the following pages to organize your scores. Comparing the scores from different groups of people participating in the assessment—such as employees, managers and customers—will give you a more balanced, accurate set of data to assess. When giving this assessment to your customers, you will need to edit or delete some of the questions they cannot answer, such as those that refer to internal business practices.

Questionnaire Results

Group: Employee

Science: Nine Sub-Categories   Sub Total

Quality of Product   _____
Product or Service Knowledge   _____
Working Environment   _____
Working Conditions: Equipment   _____
Policies and Standards   _____
Problem Solving: Knowledge   _____
Customer Support: Actions   _____
Training: Technical / Policy   _____
Quantity Performance: Efficiency   _____

Science: Total Score   _____

Group: Employee

Art: Nine Sub-Categories   Sub Total

Quality of Delivery   _____
Product or Service Knowledge   _____
Working Environment   _____
Working Conditions: Teamwork   _____
Policies and Standards   _____
Problem Solving: Support   _____
Customer Support: Appreciation   _____
Training: Interpersonal / Cultural   _____
Quality Performance: Effectiveness   _____

Art: Total Score   _____

Questionnaire Results

Group: Manager

Science: Nine Sub-Categories   Sub Total

Quality of Product   _____
Product or Service Knowledge   _____
Working Environment   _____
Working Conditions: Equipment   _____
Policies and Standards   _____
Problem Solving: Knowledge   _____
Customer Support: Actions   _____
Training: Technical / Policy   _____
Quantity Performance: Efficiency   _____

Science: Total Score   ____

Group: **Manager**

Art: **Nine Sub-Categories**   **Sub Total**

Quality of Delivery   _____
Product or Service Knowledge   _____
Working Environment   _____
Working Conditions: Teamwork   _____
Policies and Standards   _____
Problem Solving: Support   _____
Customer Support: Appreciation   _____
Training: Interpersonal / Cultural   _____
Quality Performance: Effectiveness   _____

Art: **Total Score**   _____

Questionnaire Results

Group: **Customer**

Science: Nine Sub-Categories   **Sub Total**

Quality of Product   _____
Product or Service Knowledge   _____
Working Environment   _____
Working Conditions: Equipment   _____
Policies and Standards   _____
Problem Solving: Knowledge   _____
Customer Support: Actions   _____
Training: Technical / Policy   _____
Quantity Performance: Efficiency   _____

Science: Total Score   ____

Group: Customer

Art: Nine Sub-Categories   Sub Total

Quality of Delivery   _____
Product or Service Knowledge   _____
Working Environment   _____
Working Conditions: Teamwork   _____
Policies and Standards   _____
Problem Solving: Support   _____
Customer Support: Appreciation   _____
Training: Interpersonal / Cultural   _____
Quality Performance: Effectiveness   _____

Art: Total Score   _____

Are You In Balance?

Now you want to consider your score in the two areas to assess how balanced you are individually or as a team or company. Use these final questions to reflect on your answers and scores in the two categories of art and science. Use the scores from the Questionnaire Results pages you just completed to review your customer service approach. Consider individually, or discuss as a team, areas where you are in balance, where you are focusing too much on one area at the expense of another, and where you need to improve. Again, you can separate your discussions based upon responses from employee, management, and customer groups. Transfer your discussion summaries to the following worksheets.

Bringing it All Together: Science

1. Our company, division, team, or store is currently doing enough in this area to maintain a competitive edge.

Disagree		Neutral		Agree	Don't
1	2	3	4	5	Know

Comments: _____

_____

_____

_____

Bringing it All Together: Art

1. Our company, division, team, or store is currently doing enough in this area to maintain a competitive edge.

Disagree		Neutral		Agree	Don't
1	2	3	4	5	Know

Comments: _____

_____

_____

_____

Analyzing the Results

Here's where you now get to reflect on how well you have done individually, as a team, division, or company, keeping in mind these two key principles of science and art:

The Science of Customer Service:

Scientific or information-

oriented customer service

= Technical Ability

Technical ability
= Product/Service /Customer
Knowledge
+ Job Knowledge
+ Company Knowledge

The Art of Customer Service:
Artistic or emotion-oriented
customer service requires
interpersonal ability.

Interpersonal ability
= Active/Empathetic Listening
+ Sincerity
+ Apologies

In light of these two principles, how did you do? What are your strengths, weaknesses, areas of improvements—individually and as a team or company?

After you've gone through this assessment process once, plan to do this again after you have had a chance to make any changes to improve what you are doing. Do this again in a month or two, and consider setting up a regular assessment process every subsequent month or two.

This repeated review is valuable, since for most organizations achieving a delicate balance of science and art for outstanding customer service requires constant monitoring. Individuals need to not only monitor themselves, but the whole organization needs to engage in this monitoring process. Additionally, the organization itself must be committed as a whole to supporting this balanced approach, because a positive, supportive environment contributes to preserving the balance and identifying when particular individuals or teams are in or out of balance. In fact, this positive, supportive attitude throughout the organization is so crucial, that the next section is devoted to describing the seven "must have" elements of this attitude which you need individually and throughout the organization for success.

One of the key components for maintaining the balance rests with the environment in which people work. A positive, supportive environment lends itself to the continuous, and relatively easy task of recognizing if individuals, or the team itself, is in balance or out of balance. A fundamental of outstanding service, which provides the foundation for a balanced approach, is a healthy, realistic and (yes!) positive attitude. The next section focuses on the seven absolute "must have" attitudes.

Part 2

You Gotta Have Attitude:
The Seven Absolutes

"You can't make a silk purse out of a sow's ear." You've heard this saying before, haven't you? You can't create anything of quality from poor, shoddy materials. This adage is never more true than in customer service. Doesn't matter how some employees dress up or are trained or coached with service skills, they will still upset and irritate many customers. They just don't have what it takes to become outstanding service providers, at least without a major transformation. They need to change their outlook. They need that positive, customer-friendly attitude to create rapport, much like a user-friendly computer interface provides customer appeal. Without a positive attitude, all the training and skills practice in the world are a waste of time and money. You simply GOTTA HAVE ATTITUDE—the RIGHT attitude to develop customer rapport.

As described in the previous chapter, you, as a service provider, are continually engaging in a science and art balancing act, in which you combine informational skills and interpersonal emotional abilities. Without this combination, you are out of balance. The result is poor customer service. This art/emotional side is especially difficult to learn because it's so intangible. But you can better achieve success on this art/emotional side with the right attitude. It's this attitude which lays the foundation for this side of the service equation, much like silk threads make it possible to create that silk purse. Essentially this attitude fashions the first building blocks from which the Art and Science of good service grows. You absolutely must have this attitude. Composed of seven absolutes, consistently good service is not possible without them. Have these attitudes and you can salvage even difficult, seemingly hopeless situations.

The seven attitude absolutes you must have to succeed in providing customer service are:

• Be **empathetic** and **other-centered**, so you can put yourself in the other person's shoes.

• Be **improvement oriented**, so you are striving for continuous improvement, and unwilling to "rest on your laurels."

• Have a **determination to please**, so you want to delight the customer and do the unexpected to achieve customer satisfaction.

• Have a **positive attitude,** sporting a smile and an optimistic outlook.

• Have a **curiosity and love of learning,** so you think "I'll find out" rather than "I don't know."

• Have an **ability to anticipate and take initiative**, so you work to anticipate the customer's likely questions and prepare in advance to answer them.

• Create an **environment of team care** so that you continually support the internal customer.

Mixed together, this bundle of attitudes forms the foundation on which to build the necessary technical or product training. From this you can provide excellent, balanced customer service. This section will show you how to develop and apply these seven attitude absolutes. Maybe you think you already know them. Read on anyhow. The following exercises will help you pinpoint behaviors which exhibit these qualities, so you can coach others.

Chapter 5

Attitude #1: Be empathetic and other-centered

So you're going to be a service provider? **Empathy** and **other-centeredness** go with the territory. You absolutely have to want to serve others and you have to be concerned about others to be able to serve them.

By contrast, self-centered people never make great service providers because they put their own interests and job needs first. I'm sure you can think of examples. There's the salesperson more interested in carrying on a personal phone conversation than waiting on a customer at the counter. Or how about the clerk daubing on make-up, not even aware she is offending others with something she should complete in the restroom?

Anther example of self-centeredness is the employee who fails to respond promptly to customer e-mail messages, more interested in exchanging e-mails about office politics. There are employees who cut customers short because they would rather talk than listen. Have you ever been a customer of a self-centered service provider? You probably felt irritated or disrespected, and were inclined to turn elsewhere for better service.

To be a good customer service provider, you need the Number One Attitude of focusing on others. Let your own importance fade into the background while on the job. At times, this desire to serve can be difficult even with the best of intentions, such as when you are facing a difficult, demanding customer and find the customer gets on your nerves. If the problem continues, you may feel increasingly upset. You may be close to losing your patience and control. That's because you see the situation from your own point of view. It seems like the customer is intruding on your personal space. You have been explaining what to do quite reasonably, so why doesn't the customer listen and understand, rather than just make more demands?

Look at how you can experience these situations. Call on your empathy or other-centered way of perceiving and you'll be able to step outside of your own perspective and see things from the customer's viewpoint. You'll put yourself in your customer's shoes so you can sense what he or she is thinking. When you try this, you won't be so likely to take the problem personally and blame the customer for his or her actions. Of course, some customers are completely out of line and need to be dealt with using strategies jointly developed by management and employee teams. This was discussed in Chapter 2 in the section covering apologies. With that said, strive to see things as the customer does and you're naturally more sensitive to the customer's wants and needs. You will be better able to deal with almost any situation, including two of the most difficult and common ones—the angry customer and the stupid question.

Dealing with the Angry Customer

When you deal with the angry customer, your empathy will help you consider what your customer experienced that led him or her to feel angry. While the anger may be due to a bad experience with your company's product or service—a common subject of complaint—this anger may have roots somewhere else. The outward anger is more like a symptom of other thoughts, feelings, and experiences. For example, before strolling into your store, resort, office or before contacting you via telephone, the customer may have experienced any of the following:

A late flight	Getting lost
A traffic ticket	A bad night's sleep
Sick kids	Forgetting money
An argument	A lost reservation
Too many errands	A long wait
Lousy weather	Just one of *those* days
A hectic day	Lost luggage or mail

Or...you fill in the blanks.

Whatever it is, your customer comes to you in less than prime shape. Now to top that off, your customer has a bad experience with your product or service. Or maybe you're just the next person the customer confronts, so whatever you say or do triggers an explosion.

In these situations, self-centered service providers respond defensively as soon as an angry customer confronts them. That's because they assume the attack is directed at them. By contrast, an empathetic other-centered employee can see the customer's anger in less personal terms. This service provider feels comfortable letting customers vent their emotions. Once the customer is calmed down and rapport established, the empathetic employee can work with the customer to resolve the situation.

How do you stack up? Are you that empathetic service provider? Guess what? Sometimes you can even turn an angry customer's or employee's day around completely through your empathetic and understanding response. You can transform the customer's feelings from mad to glad. Now being empathetic doesn't mean being complacent and letting people walk all over you. Actually, using empathetic understanding to effectively address what the angry person is upset about puts you in a very powerful position. You then are in control of the situation, not the angry person.

Dealing with the "Stupid" Question

Being empathetic or other-centered can help you better respond to stupid or ridiculous questions. You can look at the question in a different way. As a self-centered provider, you may consider the questions stupid or think anyone would. That's because it's how YOU experience the question. From the customer's point of view, the question may make perfect sense.

Okay. So maybe there's no way for you to see the question as other than brainless. But if you step into the customer's shoes to see the question from his perspective, you can better deal with the question in a helpful, supportive way. That's a plus for the customer who is bound to feel satisfied because you have provided a helpful answer, rather than leaving the customer feeling DUMB or diminished.

Why is this person asking what seems to be a dumb question? When you look at things from your customer's perspective you may start to understand why. As a result, you will feel more supportive in providing a reasonable, helpful answer. Often people who are flustered ask ridiculous questions because of their confusion. And you'll start to understand this as you bring empathy to your job.

This happened daily when I worked at Disneyland. Most likely it's still happening. During the busy summer season, the parade would march down Main Street at 3:00 each afternoon. Brochures handed out at the ticket booths promised this event. A recorded message broadcast over the loudspeakers at the main gate reminded park guests of that fact. Even so, at about 2:30 every day, frenzied customers all over the park would approach employees who were working at merchandise locations, on the rides, or as part of the custodial crew. The question would be quite simple: "What time does the three o'clock parade start?"

Well, you wouldn't be surprised to learn that the employees commonly found the question annoying. They were peppered with so many questions all day. And their work may have been physically draining, like the street sweepers picking up trash dumped by the Guests on a hot smoggy day when the temperature climbed to 100. The high smog level stung their eyes while more than 70,000 people milled around dumping trash all over. But Disney employees were trained to have a customer-centered response, by maintaining their composure and answering each Guest, *as if that was the first time they had ever heard that question.* They were taught to smile and say calmly something like: "The parade will start in approximately 20 minutes, at three o'clock, and I'd suggest you pick a spot along the parade route early, so you have a good view."

This customer-centered response was a winner. Customers were pleased. They enjoyed their time at Disney. Most didn't even realize their question seemed dumb. It probably seemed reasonable. A scheduled parade can be delayed. The printed schedule listing could be inaccurate. Whether the question was dumb or not, the Disney employees were taught to have this empathetic other-oriented response. This way they would treat the customer as the customer wanted to be treated. So they answered the question as helpfully as possible, regardless of their own perception of the question. They were taught to take the customer's point of view.

No matter what business you are in, you are bound to get some stupid questions. Often about things which are very obvious things to you but not necessarily to your customers. Take the employee at the deli who is often asked, "What kind of sandwiches do you have?" Reasonable question, except when the menu is posted in large letters on the wall behind the employee. Or think about the newly hired employee who interrupts your train of thought to ask "where's the restroom?" when he's standing right next to it.

Every time you get a stupid question, consider how it may not be at all unreasonable to the person asking. For instance, the customer who asks the deli clerk about the sandwiches may not be wearing glasses, so he can't read the menu. Or maybe the customer is rushing and hasn't noticed the wall. That new employee may need assurance that the door that says "Restroom" is the restroom for employees of his or her sex and seeks confirmation to avoid making an embarrassing mistake. Often these seemingly stupid questions come from people who are simply not paying attention. Even so, good customer or employee relations demands one overlook a lack of awareness anyway.

A Formula for Good Customer and Employee Relations

There's an oversupply of angry-at-the-world customers or customers with stupid questions. You can count on that. And you can count on having these people show up when you are working. Knowing how to handle these especially difficult customers is the mark of true professional. This is where you earn your "Angel of Service" wings for performing outstanding customer service. Here are suggestions how best to best deal with difficult customers.

To Handle the Angry Customer

First of all, remember the anger has nothing to do with you (at least most of the time, unless you had some previous difficulties with this customer). Whatever the case, don't take the customer's anger or hostile comments personally. If you allow negative comments to get under your skin, your ability to deliver service will suffer. You'll probably respond with anger or hostility and the conflict will escalate.

The key to successful dealings with the angry customer is to respond with empathy and caring. While the specific strategies will differ depending on the problem and the customer's personality, culture, and personal needs and wants, your first step is to put yourself in your customer's shoes and evaluate things from his or her perspective.

To Handle the Customer Who Asks Stupid Questions

The same *put yourself in the other's shoes* advice works with customers with dumb questions, too. These customers usually ask these questions out of a lack of awareness or confusion. Who of us has not been flustered or unthinking at times? Empathize with the customer who is inattentive, overwhelmed, or otherwise clueless. When the questions come, deal with that person kindly, with understanding and a desire to help. Not only will you find the customer is usually quite appreciative, but you'll make a friend. This translates into increased customer loyalty and sales.

No one would suggest it's easy to always show empathy. Any customer service representative can be tempted to respond to a particularly annoying customer with a withering comment or sarcastic remark. At your wit's end, you may want to put the customer in his or her place or make the customer go away. But don't do that. Not ever! No way! React in a hostile way and you could put yourself or your company at risk because you insulted or were demeaning to customers.

The way to avoid this temptation is to "stand outside yourself." Use the following exercise to help you practice this visualization technique.

Exercise #1: Putting You and Your Customer in a Fishbowl

First, find a quiet place where you can relax and concentrate. Close your eyes and see yourself in the following situation:

Picture yourself in the middle of the floor, in the center of a huge arena. This arena is the largest basketball or performance hall you have ever seen. As you look around in the dim light, you notice the seats in the arena are full.

Now, look straight ahead at your customer. You see that you and your customer are the only people on the floor. Suddenly a spotlight flares on, illuminating you and your customer. Another spot now lights up the stands, and among the spectators, you can see your boss, subordinates, co-workers, managers, CEO, and stockholders, as well as your father, mother, children, or other important family members.

Your customer makes an angry statement or asks a stupid question and you are tempted to tell the customer off. You want to say exactly what you think about the customer.

Then you remember all the familiar faces in those stands who are watching and listening closely for your response. You think about all the ways these people know you. They buy your products, pay your salary, write your performance reviews, look up to you, and so on.

With that on your mind, decide what you will say to that customer. How will you substitute what you would like to say with a more diplomatic, polite approach? Take a few minutes to imagine your response and how it feels to control your initial reactions.

After you finish the exercise, reflect on the experience. Entertaining thoughts that you are center stage while working with the difficult customer is a sobering way to help you shape your attitude toward your customer. When others are watching, you want to be your best. You want to show you are in control and responsive to your customer's needs and wants. Remember this feeling! Carry it with you and you can stay focused on dealing with customers with objectivity, no matter how angry, annoying, or dumb their behavior seems. This attitude will also help you respond coolly and professionally and you'll provide the highest caliber of service you can.

Exercise #2: Taking Your Customer's Point of View

Now that you've starred as yourself in a customer service drama, it's time to change characters. This exercise will help you take the customer's point of view. Imagine for a few minutes that you are a new customer and looking at the customer service provider (you). Now watch this customer service provider conducting business with the customer who is also YOU. You are in both roles now, the service provider and recipient. Ask yourself the following questions and answer them as you the customer might. Take notes as you ask these questions or write down your answers after the exercise.

- How are new customers' calls handled? Do you feel like the customer service person really cares about you? Do his or her words or actions support this feeling? If so, what has the customer service rep done to convey this attitude? If not, why not? What words or actions are disturbing to you?
- If customers come to your company, how easy is it to find the business? Is there a clear sign or road to the building or is there a maze of freeway exits and turns that might be confusing? Is there plenty of parking or are there problems finding spaces at certain times of day?

• If customers access the company via the Internet, how easy is it to use the website? If the communication is by telephone, can customers get a "live person" or do they get stuck in a series of endless, voice-mail-jail recordings from which they can't escape?
• What is the first impression you have as a customer coming through the door? Do you like the look of the store? Or is there anything you would change to make it more customer friendly?
• Does the flow of traffic inside the business make sense or is it confusing? If there are problems, what are they?
• When customers have questions or want to buy something, do you as a customer have to wait? Or is service quick and courteous?
• Are you the customer greeted or otherwise acknowledged when you enter this store, office, or place of business?
• If this business goes out to customers, how reliable is the sales staff in making appointments or in following up to answer questions, take orders, or make a delivery?
• Do staff members use any acronyms or industry terms that are confusing to you as an outside customer? What are they? How can they be changed?

After you record your responses to these questions, reflect on your answers as a customer. Notice if there are any problems in your service approach that should be changed. If so, think about how you might change them. Give yourself a week, then try this exercise again and notice the differences. Repeat the exercise on a weekly basis for at least one month. Your responses from the perspective of the customer will become increasingly positive as you improve your customer service approach.

Encourage your staff members or other team members to go through this exercise too. Or you can do this exercise in a group, followed by a group discussion.

Exercise #3: The Anonymous Customer: Conducting a Service Test

Imagination can only go so far. Besides *imagining* what it's like to be a customer observing yourself, as in the previous exercise, try a real life experiment. Enlist the help of a friend, or employee from a different department. Have that person visit your business, be a customer, and then, after observing you in action, answer the questions in the previous exercise. This is actually a good check to undertake periodically. If you don't find a friend or business associate available for this test, you may want hire a consultant to experience the service you, your department, or your company offers. Some of the most effective feedback can come from these "anonymous shoppers." Their feedback will be honest and give you a clearer idea of what a new customer experiences in your department or company. Consider having them grade your service using the categories you just used in the previous exercise or the Science/Art Questionnaire from Part I.

Chapter 6

Attitude #2: Be improvement oriented
Lessons from Disney

The next key attitude you need is being **improvement oriented.** This means you must be always ready to learn and to execute your job better and better.

In some companies, leaders and employees have a "take it or leave it" mentality. "This is the way we are. Deal with it," seems to be the attitude. When this accept-us-regardless attitude is combined with a we-know-best superiority, there's going to be trouble. An elitist, we-are-always-right attitude can backfire and cost you customers, no matter how good your product or service. Over time, customers will start leaving, since they resent this arrogant approach. Customer service reps might think, "Listen, Mr. Customer, if you don't like the service, there's the door. We have plenty of other people clamoring for our product, so we don't need to take time to deal with a few complainers like you." This attitude is never articulated but it can be felt. The more customers sense this attitude, the more likely they'll be to leave.

This might be labeled a "sacred cow" attitude. And this needs to be ripped out and replaced with an improvement-oriented approach, based on realizing that every company has things to learn. Put this sacred cow attitude out to pasture. It conveys a tone of snobbish arrogance and it can come from managers, sales people, and customer service reps. Customers with questions, problems, or complaints are viewed as an annoyance. These customers are treated as if they should consider themselves fortunate to do business with the company or the individual employee. Needless to say, customers find this approach offensive and demeaning.

This attitude is most deeply rooted in businesses selling a product or service with snob appeal. Or it's found where a company has a monopoly or near monopoly on a desirable product or service. Customers may put up with this "better than thou" attitude—for a while. If they value the product or service enough. But this won't last for long. Eventually customers will feel angry at this treatment and they will leave for other companies. This arrogance may lead to a company's downfall.

Books about business history are chock full of company has-beens that rose to glory on some innovation, thought they owned the market, and treated their customers arrogantly. These soon faded into oblivion, when competitors appeared offering a similar product or service with a smile. "Sacred cows" aren't limited to attitudes; they can also be products, policies, or people that have enjoyed a certain amount of success and the respect that accompanies it. Left alone, sacred cows often turn into untouchable icons of the past. A company can fall into this know-it -all, we-don't-need-to-learn attitude. This may be an "if it ain't broke, don't fix it" mindset which develops into an "even if it's broke, don't mess with it because it's been around for a long, long time" mantra. This paves the way for a dinosaur product or company.

Even the Walt Disney Company was not immune to this problem. I observed this during the late 1970s and early 1980s when I was at Disney. Things had been going well, at least so it seemed. But the company nearly collapsed before its rescue in the mid 1980s. The near disaster happened even though Walt Disney often admonished the troops to "never rest on your laurels," because Disney's employees began doing precisely that—resting. They came to take the customer for granted with a "we know what's best" arrogance. After all, Disney had been the leader in family entertainment for decades. There was no competition. Top managers whittled away at costs in areas they thought didn't matter.

At Disneyland, the mountain climbers on the Matterhorn were let go. Top management decided they didn't add much entertainment value or return on investment relative to the cost of their salaries and liability insurance. The original Tinkerbell retired. "Don't replace her," management dictated. And Disneyland remained a safe, clean, enjoyable place to visit. But it started to lose more and more of its magic.

They were on top, so executives at Disney didn't worry about the diminishing magic. But other companies noticed. They whittled away at Disney's customer base. At the same time, new competition poked its head up in unexpected places and ways. Giant shopping malls sprang up, which turned into entertainment centers, with lots of free window shopping and no parking and entrance fees. Some malls even offered fun rides for kids. Families eagerly responded to these lower-cost recreational opportunities closer to their homes. Easier and cheaper than to take that trek to Disneyland. Year-by-year through the late 1970s and early 1980s, attendance levels didn't rise as they should have.

Other Problems

It wasn't just the park that was suffering. The top management of the Disney Studios seemed oblivious to the growing challenge. They continued to look back to the past rather than ahead. Creative decisions were made by asking, "What would Walt Disney think?" They stopped being truly creative, since they stopped paying attention to what customers wanted and stopped taking risks. Yet both of these elements were a critical part of Walt Disney's approach. Repeatedly, he pushed creative limits with new forms of entertainment. He championed animated features with sound. But the Disney Studios floundered with two unimaginative and unsuccessful approaches to filmmaking. First, they repackaged old successes and turned out tired sequels to movies like *Herbie the Love Bug*. They hired older actors no longer popular with the younger generation. Second, new films like *Tron* and *The Black Hole* aimed to attract a new generation of viewers, but they lacked interesting plot lines to go along with their innovative special effects. Box office bombs didn't change things. Disney management refused to recognize Disney had lost its competitive edge and was no longer at the forefront of the entertainment industry. And while Disney plodded along on the safe, conservative route, a new breed of filmmakers with a more edgy attitude and awareness of customer interests, George Lucas and Steven Spielberg to name two, experimented with creative, new approaches. Their daring themes and technological breakthroughs produced blockbusters like *Star Wars, Raiders of the Lost Ark,* and *E.T. The Extra-Terrestrial.* These new films pushed the competition to new heights. Disney was left in the dust.

The root problem was cockiness. Anything with the Disney name on it will sell—this arrogant attitude cascaded down the ranks to front-line employees. Most employees didn't realize there was an attitude problem, while those who did were afraid to rock the boat by raising any questions.

At the Disney University, I experienced this arrogance when I submitted a request to management to attend a seminar organized by a leadership training company. "I want to attend an 'outside' seminar just to stay up to date on the latest trends in training at other companies and in other industries, " I explained. "Denied." This was the response stamped on my request. I needed no training, management determined. "We're Disney. They ought to learn from us."

Front-line employees were negatively impacted by this arrogant attitude in other ways. Disney hadn't produced a blockbuster film in many years so there weren't new products at Disney theme parks in California and Florida. A successful film is a springboard for new toy and clothing lines and new parades and rides based on the plot of the movie. Since there were no box-office hits, Guests at the Disney theme parks saw the same old tired rides and merchandise. They often complained about this to the employees in the shops.

Disney was pursuing a formula for failure. Management and employees were armed with an attitude of arrogance and an unwillingness to innovate. The company suffered from an aging product line and disgruntled customers. So Disney was evolving into a dinosaur, a relic of a past age. They were losing market share.

As a result, the company was in a weakened state, on the ropes, and ripe for a takeover. What happened over the period of about a year was a series of complicated financial dealings that took the company to the brink of a massive breakup and back. Twice corporate raiders shook up Disney's management by buying millions of dollars in Disney stock, threatening to take over the company and break it up by selling off individual divisions. They asserted that the company wasn't being run effectively and that the stock was undervalued as a result. Before the breakup occurred, a member of the Disney family, tired of seeing the decline of the company his family founded, attracted a group of investors (a so-called "white knight" group) interested in keeping the company intact. The investor group bought back the shares of stock from the raiders for a multi-million dollar "ransom." A subsequent huge management shake-up introduced a new CEO, president, and management team with entertainment industry know-how and the willingness to take the risks to remain competitive.

Such an arrogant, self-important attitude that nearly brought down Disney is devastating for employees in any company. It can undermine not only a myopic manager who believes he or she is invincible, but also a front-line employee who thinks that he has so much important information or that his performance is so superior that no one will ever fire him. Steeped in these delusions of grandeur and of being irreplaceable, such an employee is apt to treat even coworkers like lowly underlings, while completely ignoring anyone beneath him unless giving orders.

These stories prove that the process of decline due to arrogance occurs because:

Arrogance Leads to Complacency which Leads to Eventual Failure Unless Changed

We're talking about inevitability here. This "we're great and invincible" attitude undermines both the individual and the company. Not only does it inspire a negative reaction from others; it also stymies growth. It impedes a commitment to improving. With this arrogant attitude, you think you are already great. You don't need to do anything more. All you want is for people to acknowledge and honor you for your presumed greatness based on past achievements. This quickly turns people off and soon undermines any claim to greatness. You get stuck in an endless movie reel loop with this kind of attitude. It keeps replaying and replaying, until the film finally breaks, now too old and frayed. Or to look at it another way, when you have an arrogant attitude, you quickly wear out your welcome even if you were once a favored guest.

Exercise 4: The Arrogance or Complacency Check

Do you or does your company lack an improvement orientation because you think you're great the way you are? Have you or has your company become arrogant or complacent, the two big improvement killers? To make sure you aren't falling into the complacency-arrogance trap, take a look around. Try to spot any place these attitudes might be undermining the continuous improvement process. To help identify problem spots and determine how well you are doing, ask yourself a few questions:

You've got problems . . . if you say yes to any of these:

• Does any employee feel he or she has earned his or her spot and doesn't need to work to maintain it? Does any department feel this way?

• Do you see customer service providers showing any evidence of customer neglect by their actions or attitude?

• Do you see any signs that employees think: "We're doing great, so we don't have to do any better."

• Are any successful product lines getting outdated while you're not taking steps to replace or upgrade them?

• Do employees refrain from criticizing products, policies, or people for fear of upsetting the "Sacred Cow?"

You're doing well . . . if you say yes to these:

• Do you and your staff seek to continually learn and improve?

• Do you and your staff continually assess the competitive and user-friendliness of your current policies and procedures for dealing with customers?

• Are you and your staff keenly aware of the competition and the possibility of losing market share? What are you doing to keep this loss of share from happening?

• Do you remember to adapt your approach to customers from different backgrounds?

• Are you getting feedback from customers with different backgrounds and using it to adapt your product lines, approaches to services, and policies to better respond to these customers?

Examine your answers. Remember, there's no right or wrong, no good or bad answer, since you are assessing where you are now and what problems you need to overcome. If you or your team answered "yes" to any of the items in the "problem" column, examine how that negative attitude influences teamwork, employee relations, product quality, and, of course, customer service. Think about ways to improve your product, service, or teamwork. Don't just *think* about possibilities. Get out and start talking to your customers, employees, vendors, and subordinates to learn what *they* think needs improvement. This way you get off your pedestal and go back to the grass roots of customer service through finding out what your customers really want, including what they would like to see changed and improved. The next step? Deliver what they want.

These need to be your slogans: "Improvement" and "Watch Me Improve." People have short memories. You need a strategy to combat it. The key to a *short memory strategy* is to let customers know you are continually changing and improving. Even if you and your company have been great in the past, you don't have a mystical "right" to customer or employee loyalty. No person or organization is assured a competitive superiority forever. You and your company must work to keep that greatness. You have to earn it again and again. And to keep earning you have to keep learning. You must be willing to constantly assess your quality of service, then make the necessary changes to improve.

The best approach is early change. As soon as you notice new trends in your industry or that customers are starting to want something more—this is the time to change.

Making the changes later on is usually more expensive and painful. Let things go too long and you're like the farmer whose horse has kicked his way out of the barn and then broken down the fence on his way to a greener pasture. This farmer has to build a new barn and new fences and get a new horse. Much easier for him had he taken care of the unruly horse before the destruction.

Chapter 7

Attitude #3: Have a determination to please

Having a **determination to please** by delighting the customer and doing the unexpected will win customer kudos. No matter how old they are, people love treats and surprises. Just like doing an unexpected act of kindness will cheer someone up, doing something nice and unexpected for your customers will light them up. They like to be treated royally and **pleasantly** surprised. Find ways to delight your customers, along with providing good service, and you'll be building a base of loyal customers.

You can make a customer feel good in hundreds of small, inexpensive ways. Here is just a quick list of examples of how some people do that:

- restaurants which give a flower to every woman on Valentine's Day
- salespeople who follow up with promised phone calls
- managers who personally welcome new employees to the department
- bank tellers who use your name during a transaction

- clerks who approach you when you look lost or confused and offer to help
- operators who ask "would mind being put on hold," then <u>wait</u> for your response.

All of these approaches can make the customers feel special. I experienced this customer-pleasing treatment one day at an airport bar, when a bartender far exceeded my expectations. I was waiting for a flight (of course) and got pulled into a football game on TV. The bar was crowded. Both were strong teams. The bartender was nearly swamped, serving high-profit, alcoholic drinks.

I ordered a coffee.

"Coming right up," the bartender replied cheerfully. He pushed a full mug in front of me.

"Do you have any non-fat milk?" I asked.

"No," he answered quickly.

"That figures," I told myself, before realizing he was still talking.

"I'm sorry, we only have cream, but I think I have a solution. Right next door is a cafeteria that sells non-fat milk. If you wouldn't mind, since I'm the only one at the bar, feel free to go there and grab a small carton. And there's no need to pay. Just tell them I sent you. Then, leave what you don't use on the bar, and I'll take care of the charges."

I was more than delighted. Amazed, in fact, since the last place I expected good service was in an airport bar. Both bars and airports have a reputation for harried customer service providers dealing rapidly with a stream of fast-moving or demanding customers. Here I was with my one-dollar cup of coffee, while most of the other customers were buying drinks costing several dollars—and leaving larger tips. But the bartender treated me as if I was just as valuable as a higher-paying customer. He was attentive, smiled, and gave me an option to help myself to the non-fat milk if I didn't want my coffee black. As I watched him, I saw he was treating everyone else with the same friendly, helpful attitude. He seemed to be having a great time as he smiled and joked with customers! He had a determination to please, and it not only pleased the customers, but himself as well. He was demonstrating the essence of a balanced approach: he was both friendly and very efficient. And both he and his customers benefited from it. In spite of the rushed environment, we were all enjoying ourselves.

If that overworked airport bartender could accomplish such customer delight with his creativity and good spirits, you and your team should be able to similarly delight your customers. The following exercise will help employee teams find new ways to exceed customers' expectations. And you'll improve your team or work group morale as you do.

Exercise 5: Thinking of Ways to Delight Your Customer

How do you and your team delight your customers? To find out, organize a team meeting to explore all the ways you and your team have done so. Consider the idea of "customer" in very broad terms. Think about both internal and external customers. And then pay attention to customers from different cultures. Use the chart on the following page to guide you. If you are doing this in a group, there are two approaches. You can discuss these strategies as a group and ask one person to write down the responses as you go along. Or you can make a copy of a chart for each person to write down individual responses. Reconvene then to compare and discuss your answers.

If you are leading the group, ask everyone to state or write down the strategies they have found effective for delighting customers. These strategies should be described as specific actions followed by a description of how the customer reacted to display his or her pleasure. Next to each strategy and customer response, write down the costs of the action, including both the out-of-pocket costs for the giveaways or the cost of the employee's pay for the time taken in providing this service. (Use the employee's hourly rate of pay to figure out the amount for the time taken.) In the fourth column, write down the ways this satisfaction might contribute to the company's success. Even if you can't measure this success now, note what you think the contribution might be.

Do a cost-benefits comparison after you write up the results. You will notice how little these special customer treats usually cost the company—especially when measured against the customer's pleasure, increased loyalty, and future sales that are likely results.

Benefits

Costs

Employee Pay

Out-of-Pocket

Strategies Delighting the Customer

Here are some of the benefits you can expect from doing this exercise.

1. Your team will have tons of ideas on how to delight your customers. You can save and use many of these over the coming months.

2. The process of looking for ways to please the customer will dramatically increase your team or department's morale. It's kind of like a game.

3. As you put these ideas into practice, you will increasingly delight your customers and exceed their expectations. Your results will be increased customer goodwill and more business. This leads ultimately to a better bottom line.

You'll discover that the return on a minimal investment of goodwill more than pays for your investment in these efforts through an increase in happy, repeat customers and a staff that gets better and better, as everyone looks for ways to outperform themselves in the future. So everyone wins—you, the customer, and the company—and the business thrives.

Chapter 8

Attitude #4:
Have a positive attitude
Sweeping on Mainstreet

Another key to outstanding service is to have that **positive attitude**—or look like you have it, even when you don't feel it. That means thinking about situations in a positive way. A positive thinker regards problems as situations to be resolved rather thazn as conflicts, difficulties, or hurdles to overcome.

Like most service providers, you may have those days when you would rather be *anywhere else* doing *anything else* than providing service to *anyone*. But service champions have a trick for overcoming those glum days, much like top salespeople approach each sale with energy and enthusiasm regardless of how they feel that day. The trick is this: they plaster a big smile on their face, tell themselves they feel great (a little self-talk here to accompany that smile), and then they go out and sell.

Try it. Smile right now. A big smile. Notice how it immediately perks you up? You simply can't be depressed while holding a big smile. Tough to feel blue when you look chipper and happy. The longer you keep smiling, the harder you'll find staying down becomes. Just put a smile on your face and see.

Maybe a big happy smile isn't appropriate where you work. Or perhaps you're still developing that outward cheerful look. A good way to feel positive inside is to *picture* yourself smiling in your mind. That vision will help you create the corresponding feeling so you glow inside and can better express that to others. In turn, when you smile at others, even slightly, people will generally respond back positively. Try an experiment. Consciously smile at people for the day and see what happens. Count the number of smiles and pleased responses you get back. You'll most likely get so many more pleasant responses than when you don't think about this. Well, this is hard to measure, since when you aren't consciously smiling, you aren't counting!

A fake smile is not the solution to all your problems. But consider the alternative. If you don't have a positive attitude, you will probably turn off customers, but that's not all. Situations at work each day are more likely to get you down and you will find yourself in a negative spiral. Repetitive situations can be exasperating. Those same old "stupid questions," like "what time is the three o'clock parade?" can drive you crazy. When I worked as a trainee with the Disney street-sweeping crew and heard that question again and again, I let my annoyance get me down instead of finding something enjoyable about the job. On top of feeling stressed and irritated, I spent my breaks and lunch hours complaining about "those people" to my co-workers. As you might expect, my complaints only made my situation worse. It alienated me from my co-workers. Nobody wanted to join me for lunch and breaks. They were tired of hearing me moan and groan.

You can always change such a negative attitude. I did. With help. A long-time employee who had become a friend advised me to change my poor attitude if I wanted to enjoy the job and get along.

"I don't think I can do that," I said.

"I betcha," he said.

"What?"

"I bet you $5 you can't get 180 stupid questions in one day from the customers," he said.

Taking the Bet

It was a dumb bet, I thought, but I was sure I could win. Even if it was a dumb idea. And I was also intrigued by the spirit of the game and by the notion that if his crazy idea worked, I would gain tremendous benefits.

Next day, armed with my broom and dustpan, I started to tally all the stupid questions I got during my shift. I used a small clicker-type counter which I kept in my pocket and clicked after each stupid question.

Click, click. At first, as I swept, I had the usual negative thoughts about people who didn't read signs and dumped their trash anywhere but in the trash containers. But after I didn't get a stupid question for 20 minutes, I felt motivated to take some action to get 180 stupid questions by the end of my shift. Click, click, click. Instead of just looking at the ground while sweeping, I started *looking up at the customers.* The change was dramatic. I started to hunt for customers who appeared lost, confused, or in need of help **... potential clicks!** They might have a stupid question to ask me, I thought. Oh, there was a family puzzling over a park map.

"Can I help you find something?" I asked with a smile. I was delighted at their question. "Where is the entrance to Frontierland?" They were standing right next to it!

You can probably guess what happened. As I searched for customers with stupid questions to help, I completely lost my negative attitude about stupid customers. Instead, I found I enjoyed the game of approaching and talking to customers so much that I lost track of how many questions I collected. Well, I lost $5 that day because I only got 150 clicks, not 180. But I won an unforgettable lesson—the importance of having a positive attitude in customer service. Not only did I stop complaining to co-workers during breaks and lunch—at the end of each shift, I was bursting with energy. Taking care of my customers and giving them joy by paying attention to them and their needs had a boomerang effect. That joy came right back to me. Their delight in turn delighted me. I started feeling even more positive about my customers and my new way of relating to them. In turn, many customers complimented me for going out of my way to help them. I gloried in those compliments. My balanced approach gave me the energy to be more attentive to my customers, co-workers and myself. We all benefited.

No matter what the situation, you can discover a way to have a positive attitude in whatever you are doing. This positive outlook will pay off many times over—both in making your customer feel good and making you feel good as well. You can even develop your own "mental clicker" to transform your attitude from negative to positive. Even when I wasn't clicking away those stupid questions, the idea of the clicker changed my focus and attitude at Disney. All I had to do was picture myself going "click" when I encountered a difficult customer or situation. Later I did this mental clicking in other jobs. Whenever I felt over-whelmed by customer complaints or demands, I would imagine myself clicking away. Then my attitude quickly changed from negative to positive.

Exercise 6: Finding Ways to Stay Positive with Your Own Mental Clicker or Other Games

You can create your own mental clicker or similar games to make fun of a dull or difficult situation. You'll not only enjoy what you are doing more, but your customers and other employees will respond to you more positively.

A way to stay positive as a group is to allocate time at your regular staff meetings to share how you each handled your "crazy questions of the week." Discuss what strategy you each used to answer the question and maintain your positive attitude. Invite everyone to discuss ideas, even really wacky ones, on how to keep a positive attitude.

Notice what happens when you try mental clicking. Maybe it's looking for the best crazy question of the day, or some other games for a day, or a week, or a month. You are virtually assured of positive results.

Sharing Your Positive Outlook with Your Customers
You need to go beyond thinking positively and looking positive with that smile. Share your positive outlook with customers by what you say. Be prepared to reframe any problem into a challenge or situation to be handled, and handle it with that can-do mindset. Your customers will love you for it.

EVEN MONKEYS FALL FROM TREES

That's what a VP and Premier Banker at a major bank did. Let's call her Karla. And that's why Karla was promoted to that position from her branch manager job. Her attitude with disgruntled customers was to see them not as having a problem, but rather a situation to be handled. This attitude helped her approach customers in a much more positive way. That's exactly what happened when one frustrated customer came into the bank to ask about an unexpected $20 checking account charge. As Karla was completing a transaction with one customer, she overheard another customer, let's call him Dan, complain to an assistant bank manager.

"I don't know where this $20 came from," he said. "I shouldn't have been charged that fee. My balance was well over the minimum amount necessary for free checking."

The assistant bank manager poured over the bank statement. "Who can I see about discussing this problem?" Dan asked, as the assistant bank manager hesitated, wondering whether she could handle this herself. But before she could answer, Karla sidled up to Dan, smiled broadly, and said, "I can see that you're concerned. How can I help?" A few minutes later she had resolved the problem completely. A computer error was responsible for the fee, because Dan did have more than adequate amounts in his premier checking account. Within minutes, Karla had uncovered the source of the "situation to be handled" and had reversed the charge. In fact, she checked further and discovered a $20 charge on Dan's upcoming statement, which he hadn't yet received. She reversed that charge too. Of course, a $20 charge for a premier checking customer like Dan wouldn't devastate his financial stability. That's not the point. It is the <u>principle,</u> not the monetary amount and Karla knew this. Her approach was balanced in that she solved his problem and she exhibited a friendly, empathetic approach.

Dan was delighted both with her positive can-do attitude and with her quick follow-through to resolve the situation. At no point was Dan turned into the "bad guy" as so often happens. Given this attitude, it's no wonder Karla was promoted to a vice president level to work with the bank's premier customers with the largest accounts. She had the ideal approach—customer service with a positive attitude.

Exercise 7: Turning Negatives into Positives Through Brainstorming

You too can develop that approach of turning negatives into positives in whatever you do so this attitude becomes a natural part of relating to customers. You won't have to think about <u>having</u> a positive attitude; it will become an inherent part of your make up.

A good way to develop or reinforce this negative into positive outlook is to regularly brainstorm turning negatives into positives. Make this process a habit. This is described in *The Empowered Mind: How to Harness the Creative Force within You*, by creativity and conflict resolution specialist Gini Graham Scott, Ph.D. She says that the goal is to think of win-win possibilities for yourself and anyone else involved in any problem situation. Use brainstorming to come up with a variety of ways to change something negative into something as beneficial as possible to all concerned. Choose the best approach from these options.

In a simple customer problem, as with the bank customer, the negative into positive solution may be immediately obvious. In more complicated cases, that may not be true.

There may be a number of possibilities, such as returning merchandise for a refund, fixing merchandise, providing new merchandise as an exchange, or doing even more if there is a systems problem effecting many customers. Whatever the problem, the key to a satisfied customer is developing an automatic negative-into-positives approach and learning to use your intuition, creativity, and ability to brainstorm good ideas.

The following exercise will help you shift your thinking. Use it individually or in a group to think about positive alternatives. Try practicing this for five to ten minutes a day, using current problems or ones you imagine might occur. Think how to reframe the problems positively and resolve them.

Get in a relaxed state with a sheet of paper in front of you to record your ideas. If you want, close your eyes. Now envision a problem situation. Make it as specific as possible. Next, ask your question, framing it in a positive, open-ended way, such as: "How many ways can I..." or "What are all the things I can do to help my customer benefit from this current situation?"

Let your mind go. Write down all the positive things you can do. When you are done, notice how many positive alternatives you've listed. Prioritize the possibilities according to how much you want to do. Divide them into A, B, and C categories, based on how much you would like to put these ideas into practice. If there are still too many ideas, prioritize in the A category. Choose what you want to do and then try it out in a real situation.

Think about it later. How can you apply the results of this exercise to help you have a positive, can-do frame of mind in each customer interaction? As you practice working with this exercise, you will discover the negative-into-positives attitude becomes second nature. You don't even need to write anything down or close your eyes to think of possibilities. You have trained yourself to think positively.

Chapter 9

Attitude #5: Have a curiosity and love of learning

Another critical customer service attitude is *wanting to know,* so you have the information you need to help. The essence of this attitude is curiosity. The attitude *I don't know and I don't want to know* is a guaranteed customer service killer. It'll make the job less fun for you, too.

This don't know, head-in-the-sand ostrich approach appears when service providers respond to questions outside of the usual customer interchange with a response such as:

- "Sorry, I don't know. Try the next window, please."
- "Gosh, no one ever asked that question before." (This is accompanied with a look of befuddlement.)
- "I don't have the answer. Why don't you call back tomorrow when the technician is in."
- "I can't help you with that. The company that supplies that part is closed on weekends."
- "Our computer system is down right now, so I can't take your order." (This response is instead of finding a way to take the order anyway.)
- "Our data center is on the West Coast and they haven't opened yet." (This is instead of suggesting

a way to handle the question now, before the center opens, or offering to call the customer back after it opens.)

The list of such comments can go on and on. They all reflect the "I don't know" and "I can't be bothered to find out" attitude, which is a common service killer. When you give the customer this response, you are essentially saying, "I don't care. It's too much work to deal with your problem, if I don't know exactly what to do. So I don't want to do it. You're on your own." And even though this attitude is not articulated directly, customers get it.

Passing the buck. That's what this kind of service provider is doing. But many customers don't want to go to someone else. They are looking to you for the answer. If you use this pass-the-buck approach when you don't know, you are abandoning your customers. You can expect that they will eventually abandon you.

What a contrast when a service provider says "I'll find out" and does so. This attitude delights customers. You show you want to do everything you can to find a way to help the customer in spite of the difficulties and your lack of knowledge right now. No matter what the problem, you're ready, willing, and able to take the initiative and do the necessary follow-up to make the customer happy. Tell the customer you want to learn what he or she wants to know, so you can help find a solution to the problem. You may even come up with a solution *before* the customer asks for it. The more sensitive you are to the customer, the more likely you are to anticipate problems and concerns.

The following scenario illustrates the difference between the employee with the "I don't know" attitude and one with the "I'll find out" approach. You'll note quite quickly which approach is more likely to create the pain of neglect and which will bring the joy through attention.

I Don't Know Because the Information Isn't Available

You've probably heard it often, this "don't know-no info" response. It's particularly common in today's high-tech environment, when the technical information or technical support provider is not immediately available. Here are two alternate ways to deal with the problem.

The "Don't Know—Don't Have a Clue" Response.
"I'm sorry. I can't help you with that. The company division that supplies that part is closed on weekends."
Now look at a different, much better way.

The "I Don't Know, But I'll Find Out" Response
"I am sorry, but the company division that supplies that part is closed today and Sunday. But I have a suggestion on what to do. I can call that division for you the first thing on Monday morning to order the part. Then I can call you to tell you when it will be available. Would that help?"

A helpful good start, but this is only a promise to follow up by an individual employee. Now that employee may not work on Mondays. You need a company-wide attitude of service, so one employee can communicate these special customer needs to the next employee in that position. With this approach, someone is always available to handle the necessary follow-up. It really doesn't matter to the customer who follows through. The customer just cares that he gets that part.

When you can't follow through due to a shift change, vacation, illness, or other reason, be prepared to respond to any situation requiring follow-up with a "I'll find out for you—or I'll make sure that someone else does" attitude. If this attitude is implemented company-wide, the needed follow-up will occur as a matter of course. For instance, the employee who takes the original message might leave the information on what to do next in a chronological time-to-call or to-do file. This way, if he or she isn't there, another employee on the shift or doing follow-up can know how to meet the first employee's offer to the customer.

For instance, in the above scenario, the employee might say something like this:

"Our company will call the order in to the supplier first thing Monday morning. Since I'll be off then, another employee on that shift, Sharon, will call you to let you know when the part you want will be available."

Generally, customers will be quite pleased with this response. They'll know you are doing the best to help when you are on the job and that you are arranging to have someone to step in when you aren't available. It will be a rare situation, but you may run across a customer who only wants *your* help. You might handle that case with a comment like this:

"I wish I could be here to make the call for you. But since I can't, I wanted to assure you that I will personally follow-up with my replacement, whose name is Sharon, to explain your situation and tell her what to do. I will talk to her before I leave today and I will point out how important it is for you to get the part. I know Sharon is very conscientious, and I'm certain she will make the call."

If you arrange for someone to follow up for you when

you are away, you can do these two things on your return:
1) Check with your co-worker to make sure she followed
through and, 2) Contact your customer to make sure everything was handled to the customer's satisfaction.

Chapter 10

Attitude #6: Have an ability to anticipate and take the initiative

This sixth key attitude is really a combination of the first five attitudes, since it builds on them to produce truly great customer service. In order to have this sixth attitude, you must be empathetic and other-centered, improvement oriented, have a determination to please, have a positive attitude, and a curiosity and love of learning. When you combine those qualities with being proactive, through *anticipating possibilities and taking the initiative*, you are ready to respond with all of these qualities. When you think ahead you can better act appropriately in a wide variety of situations.

Such advance planning is a common requirement for success in many fields. Whatever your position or industry, you need to do extensive day-to-day or long-range planning. Salespeople plan presentations, clergymen and women plan sermons, athletes develop a game plan, managers plan meetings, teachers plan curricula, and so on. There's planning to do in customer service as well. Plan for how to deal with the most likely questions, complaints, concerns, emergencies, and compliments your customers bring you. You'll be better prepared to deal with a difficult situation, even when you mess up and contribute to causing the problem, such as in the following scenario.

Oh My Gosh, We Messed Up

Even with the best of intentions, you will encounter some inevitable screw-ups. That's because we're all human and sometimes it takes a number of people working together on a task, perhaps a complicated one. A lot can go wrong. Some critical bit of information may be left out of the loop, machines can break down, the post-office doesn't deliver, or something else.

Whatever the screw-up, it can be tricky knowing what to do. Take the initiative and look for solutions. This will help a disappointed or upset customer deal with what has occurred. In fact, in these litigious times, a creative, helpful response can go a long way toward resolving dissatisfactions and hurt feelings, and avert a more serious conflict. This supportive response also preserves customer loyalty, even when you did not get things right the first time.

Just before leaving on a business trip is not when you want things to go wrong. I was rushing around with last minute details. I dropped in at my optometrist's office to pick up a pair of prescription sunglasses I had ordered. It wasn't my day. The sunglasses had the incorrect frames and the lenses were the wrong shape, although the lens prescription was correct. See if you can determine what the clerk did wrong in this situation.

The Case of the Incorrect Order

I walked right up to the counter. "Your office called and told me my prescription sunglasses were ready. I'm here to pick them up," I told the young woman at the front.

"Yes, they arrived from the lab. If you'll have a seat, we'll see how they fit."

A few minutes later, she came over with the glasses and pulled them out of their case. My mouth must have dropped open.

"Is there something wrong?" she asked.

"This isn't what I ordered," I said. But I tried them on. Fortunately the prescription was right.

"This is the wrong frame. The shape of the lens is different than the model I ordered."

She thumbed through the paperwork. "Yes, you are absolutely right. I am terribly sorry this happened. I'll send the glasses back to the lab and put a 'rush' on the order. That way we'll get them back in seven days, instead of the usual fourteen."

I shook my head. "That won't work. I ordered these glasses with plenty of time to spare, so I would have them for my trip. I leave in three days. I wanted to have them before I left. I really need them for the work I will be doing on my trip."

"Yes, Mr. Lipp, I understand," she said. "I can see you are frustrated and you have a right to be upset. We certainly want you to be satisfied, since our goal is customer satisfaction. So we'll get your sunglasses remade immediately."

Of course I wasn't satisfied. It must have shown on my face.

"I still won't have any sunglasses for my trip."

She looked a bit confused. " Why, yes, that's true."

Since she wasn't coming up with a solution, I was forced to. "Look, l have an idea. Why don't you just loan me this pair until the correct pair that you re-order arrives?"

She looked relieved. "Interesting idea. Let me check with my manager to see if I can do that. I'll be right back."

When the clerk returned with her manager, he quickly agreed with suggestion. Both the manager and clerk were appropriately concerned that their supplier hadn't processed the order correctly and were very apologetic.

So what did they do wrong? Stop just a minute to review and think about the situation, before I tell you what I think.

*   *   *

Ready to go on? So what was the problem? Mainly, the error was that the clerk didn't come up with the obvious solution to satisfy my need for usable glasses on my trip. Instead, I had to propose the satisfactory solution of borrowing the glasses until the other order arrived. The approach I suggested was reasonable. I wasn't demanding something I truly didn't deserve. But I would have felt much more pleased if the solution had come from them. And if the clerk and her manager had more of a can-do, thoughtful, take-the-initiative, how-can-we-solve-this attitude, they probably would have come up with the same solution.

Many customers would not be comfortable making such a suggestion. Some would fear looking like they were trying to get something for nothing. And other customers would have been so focused on what had gone wrong they'd have no idea on how to make it right. Also, depending on the customer's cultural background or personality style, some customers would not be assertive enough for fear of "creating a problem." They would accept whatever the service provider told them. Many customers in this situation would have left dissatisfied because they didn't get the correct product, delivered on time, and hassle-free.

It would have been so much better had the clerk taken a little initiative to problem solve. She could have quickly suggested I borrow the incorrect pair, while she reordered. Maybe it's not just the clerk's fault. The company should have anticipated how to solve this problem by developing a policy of using "mistakes" as loaners.

The good news is that both the assistant and the optometrist had the right attitude. They were both very empathetic. I appreciated the concern and cooperation, especially since this was my first time to their office and they took a loss in handling my situation. However, this loss led to more business for them, as I shared my story with several friends who later ordered glasses from them.

It's not enough to be pleasant and positive, however. Service providers need to anticipate a wide variety of problem situations and be prepared to offer solutions when these problems occur. This is a form of preventive maintenance. This will help you head off recurring or likely problems in your business, resulting in more profits and more satisfied customers—just like the preventive approach to crime can cut down on crime costs.

Many companies take more of a solve-it-when-it-happens approach. They respond after-the-fact, when customers become assertive, angry, or complain to get attention.

But that attitude is so wrong-headed. It's like greasing squeaky wheels after the accident, instead of taking the safer route of performing preventative maintenance on a regular basis to minimize the squeaks (and keep the wheel from falling off). Irate customers *whose frustrations aren't taken care of* are not likely to bring you repeat business, whereas satisfied customers, including customers whose problems have been solved, are a prime source of future business. This anticipatory/initiative-taking attitude will reduce your number of complaining customers and increase the number of satisfied ones. That means more repeat business.

Exercise 8: Turning "I Don't Know" into "Let Me Help"

The following exercise will help you adopt this more proactive approach, help you anticipate your customers' likely questions or needs, and take the initiative through advance planning on how to handle them.

Start by reviewing the two situations just introduced: the "I Don't Know Because The Information Isn't Available Now" and the "Oh My Gosh, We Messed Up" scenarios.

Next, either individually or as a team, develop a list illustrating the many ways each scenario could occur in your operation. Then, for each item, create a list of as many possible ways as you can think of to remedy the situation.

Your list will look something like this with two columns on a page:

"I Don't Know Because The Information Isn't Available Now"

Possible Situations	Possible Barriers to Solution	Possible Remedies

"Oh, My Gosh, We Messed Up"

Possible Situations	Possible Barriers to Solution	Possible Remedies

For the first scenario about lack of information, in the situations column, list the possible areas where this kind of situation might pop up. Then, in the second column, list the barriers, logjams, or blocks in your company that would prevent you from getting the information you need to answer a customer's questions right away. Brainstorm ways to overcome each of these barriers. List these possible resolutions in column three. In some cases, you may need to include other departments in your company in the process to come up with viable solutions to particular problems.

In the second, the "we messed up" scenario, think of the major types of mistakes you might make and list these in column one. Identify barriers to solving this type of problem (past, present or future) in column two. Brainstorm how to respond to those mistakes and list those possible resolutions in column three. Here you also may need to involve other departments in the process to arrive at good solutions. Determine which mistakes result in product returns or customer complaints and how to respond to them. If you do need outside input from other departments, then include them in both phases—listing mistakes and generating possible solutions.

The key to doing this process of assessing mistakes and seeking solutions is to review these scenarios individually or in a group *in advance*. Then be open to exploring new and creative approaches to problem solving.

The proactive approach demands first reflecting on yourself and those you work with to assess both your own and your team's ability to provide solutions *before* your customers do it for you. A good way to encourage this proactive mindset and the high morale it inspires is treating the process of seeking proactive solutions as a game. In some companies, groups competitively seek ways to outdo each other in getting information to the customer. Other companies offer "Solution of the Month" awards to the employee or team with the best solution to a customer's problem.

Empowerment vs. "Dumping"

Another management tip. As mentioned earlier, the key to being proactive is the feeling of *empowerment* among front-line workers. Front-line employees need to feel comfortable taking on more decision-making power, taking on more responsibility and initiative. Management gives lip service to the ideal and tells employees "Okay, you're empowered." But all too often management doesn't give these employers the authority to make major decisions or engage in proactive planning. Without a certain amount of power, a front-line employee isn't going to anticipate and take the initiative, because this requires a sense of being in control or in charge to act in this way. Not having authority undermines feeling empowered or engaging in planning. To do either of these things, employees need to know what to do in any given situation. They need to know when they can take care of the problem themselves and when to call a supervisor. They need to know when they can give away or discount a product through "comping" and how much to offer. They need to know how to handle loud or abusive customers, and so on. If employees lack authority or control to act on their plans, they may figure, "So what?" They may give up planning, anticipating, or initiating, since their ideas may just be shot down. Empowerment goes hand in hand with planning, the essential component of being proactive. If you are going to be proactive, you need to be empowered to act on your plans and your anticipated responses to possible problem situations.

Dealing with the REALLY Difficult Customer

Proactive thinking is necessary for handling a customer who is especially difficult. Once you are empowered to take such action, anticipate virtually every conceivable difficulty a customer can complain about. Next, plan out a menu of alternative acceptable solutions, so you can adapt the solution to the customer's needs. This is a time to review past interactions with customers by you and other service providers, so you can analyze your successes that resulted in pleased customers and your failures that left customers still upset. From this you can better anticipate what may happen in the future. The advantage of doing this planning and review is you avoid being surprised or caught unprepared. You are fully knowledgeable about what has worked and what hasn't in the past, so you can apply this knowledge by planning what to do, based on actual experience.

A good way to anticipate possible future problems is to look to the past. Ask your co-workers and team members how they have effectively handled difficult situations. The following exercise will help you do this. Besides giving you ideas about what to do, this exercise will also help you identify truly empowered employees who have already demonstrated the ability to use the skills of anticipating and taking the initiative. Once you identify these especially skilled, empowered, and proactive employees, other team members can use them as models. This will further increase team performance and morale.

Exercise 9: Learning from Past Examples of Anticipation and Taking the Initiative

This exercise will help you better deal with future problems by anticipating them and planning what to do. You can do this exercise individually or as a group. If you do it individually, reflect on your experiences on your own. Or if you do it with a group, everyone should follow these steps either individually or as a group, and then discuss their experiences together.

Step 1: Ask for Examples.

Ask the people who deal with customers every day for examples of the questions customers frequently ask and the difficult-to-handle situations that commonly occur. Don't limit your queries to customer service people in your own company or industry, although they are a key resource. Broaden your search to seek outside examples. You'll discover more ideas you can apply in your own company. There are many sources of external advice that could help you create a more robust list. If you or one of the people on your team belongs to volunteer organizations, seek out the opinions of fellow members in that organization. Additional sources of support can include, but are not limited to the following groups.

Professional Development Groups: There are as many of these as there are types of jobs. There are groups for engineers, administrators, trainers, health care providers, landscape architects, and public service professionals. Association with the group representing your field of expertise will expose you to industry-specific ideas.

Chambers of Commerce: Most communities have some sort of Chamber or other type of Economic Development group. These organizations usually have representatives or advisory groups made up of people from a cross-section of the business community. Examples gained here can offer you a wide range of options that you can adapt to your organization and customer base.

Community Development and Volunteer Organizations: There are many to choose from, such as Rotary International, The Lions Club, Soroptimist International, Big Brothers and Sisters, etc. The only requirement for participation is your time. These types of organizations have members from virtually every part of a community. You can gather valuable ideas from people who might actually represent your customer base.

Spiritual Advisors: Many spiritual advisors are well trained in the art of listening, counseling, and problem solving. Also, don't underestimate the business acumen many possess.

For the best results, tell the people you query that you want them to think of problems they frequently encounter as well as the solutions they find effective. Then interview them about these problems and solutions. Give them a week to prepare for the interview so they will have time to think of many different situations and solutions. You will get more information if you give them time to prepare rather than discuss experiences off the top of their head.

Step 2: Compile a List

Now create a comprehensive list of questions and situations from the data you have gathered in the interviews. Use a separate notepad and organize this list into two columns, headed "situations" and "resolutions." An example is shown below. You'll clearly see the main questions and situations that occurred and how they were resolved. This list will look something like the one described in the previous exercise, except there you were thinking about possible situations and remedies. Here you will be listing actual situations and resolutions or remedies based on your interviews. In this case, your list will look something like this:

Situations   Resolutions

_____

_____

_____

Then, as you have created your list, group the related situations and responses by category, theme, or topic most relevant to the type of service or products you provide. The number of categories is something for you and your team to decide, but here are a few examples:

- Product Returns
- Product Replacement
- Employee Error
- Cancellations (service, appointments, etc.)
- System/Product Malfunctions
- Inclement Weather
- Angry Customers
- Poor Performance of Affiliated Companies, Departments, Stores, Facilities
- Procedures for Escalating Problems to Management

Step 3: Organize and Analyze the Results

Next, personalize and prioritize the results of your interviews. If you are doing this exercise on your own, use the responses you have gathered. If you work as a group, combine your lists and analyze them together—or individually analyze your results and then share.

Take the information you generated in Step Two to a more specific level by organizing both the situations and responses you listed in order of frequency or commonality. Start with the most common or frequently occurring situation facing your company, division, location, or store. Then list the ways you have effectively dealt with that type of situation in the past, your response. Then list the next most common, and so forth. This step will help you focus on the areas where you should make immediate changes and where you will probably see the most dramatic improvements.

You should end up with a prioritized list of strategic responses for each category of situation, so the most commonly used one is first, the next most common one is second, and so on. Your results will look something like this:

Category:
(List one of the categories you determined in Step 2)

Situations	*Resolutions*
Situation #1	Effective Strategy #1
(most common)	(most common)
	Effective Strategy #2
	Effective Strategy #3
	and so on…
Situation #2:	Effective Strategy #1
(next most common)	(next most common)
	Effective Strategy #2
	Effective Strategy #3
	and so on…

This organizational process will help you see the most common situations and the most effective ways of dealing with them, whether they involve internal or external customers.

In some situations, you will find that the responses you have used in the past haven't been all that effective. In that case, it will be helpful to use the format shown below. Notice that this has a revised second column and an additional, third column: Suggested Resolutions. These will need to be identified in a brainstorming or other sort of creative problem-solving session.

Situations	Ineffective Resolutions	Suggested Resolutions
Situation #1 (most common)	Ineffective Strategy #1 (most common) Ineffective Strategy #2 Ineffective Strategy #3 and so on...	Brainstorm this
Situation #2: (next most common)	Ineffective Strategy #1 (next most common) Ineffective Strategy #2 Ineffective Strategy #3 and so on...	

As I have suggested repeatedly in this book, the strongest service providers take the time to identify both their strengths and areas to improve. These lists from this exercise alone should shine a light on both.

Step 4: Create Policies and Procedures for the Future

Now it's time to put the effective strategies into practice in your company. Organize your results from Step Three into a report or summary highlighting the major questions or situations along with the most common strategies for dealing with them. Be sure to include the most effective and least effective resolution strategies. Take this report or summary to a group of peers or to a management team for review. Propose the strategies you would like to implement in your own company and ask the relevant groups or departments for feedback about these strategies. Also ask if they agree with your recommendations on your preferred strategies and encourage them to make additional suggestions on strategies to please the customer. Also, suggest ways in which to minimize or eliminate the ineffective resolution strategies. With this feedback you can refine your suggested strategies and get cooperation from others in your company. You want to get support from as many levels of management as necessary to implement the changes suggested by your research.

Step 5: Create a Booklet on Effective Strategies

As a last step in nurturing a proactive culture, organize your findings in a polished report or booklet, either in electronic or published form, to distribute throughout your department, division or company. This summary report can guide others in the company on how to give better customer service. Give this report to new hires to help them in their initial training. Make this report as widely available as possible. The greater awareness people have of effective strategies, the more you can magnify the efforts by you and your team to give outstanding customer service throughout your organization.

Look at this report as always a "work in progress." Encourage employees to add their comments, suggestions, questions, and situations for inclusion in updated reports on a continuing basis. If you use your company's intranet to distribute an electronic version, the newest editions will be even easier to produce and share.

The advantage of this open-ended, never-finished approach is that you get additional and even better ideas for providing good customer service, plus all employees can feel they are part of the process and thus feel even more empowered. A good way to do these regular updates is to invite employees to participate in a monthly "customer service" survey in which they make suggestions. You can include the good ideas in the next monthly update of the report, whether you publish it as a book or electronically.

Chapter 11

Attitude 7: Create an environment of team care

The final must-have attitude is *being concerned about everyone on your team* so you can provide the support customer service employees need to maintain the other six attitudes. They need to feel as cared for as customers if they are to stay motivated and enthusiastic about helping and providing service. And this isn't just the responsibility of management. Of course, great management leads to great service and lousy management leads to lousy service. However, the responsibility of team-care is on everyone's shoulders. If service providers don't feel cared for themselves, or don't take care of each other, all the talk about having the right attitude is just another management flavor-of-the-month gimmick that isn't taken very seriously. If they are not cared for, they will feel poorly trained, overworked, burned with unrealistic sales goals, or otherwise under too much pressure to feel enthusiastic and motivated to serve others.

Think of what it takes be a good swimmer and create a strong swim team. If you're only a weak swimmer struggling not to drown, you won't have the energy or interest to worry whether your swim strokes look good. Before you can think about perfecting your strokes, you need the proper lessons and coaching in safe, shallow waters to feel secure in the basics of swimming. Only then will you feel comfortable enough to work on your form or improve your speed.

The same is true for customer service. Employees need to feel safe, supported, and cared for before they can feel empowered to perform at the highest levels of customer service. That's why organizations that succeed year after year in providing top-level customer service encourage, even sometimes insist, their employees to participate in training and development programs. These programs, in turn, give both employees and management a clear picture of company policy, empowerment guidelines, and under what circumstances employees can take the initiative on their own levels and appropriate actions.

Such programs make it very clear what employees can and can't do at their level of authority, so they don't have to constantly guess and worry about whether they are acting appropriately. Guidelines and training make it clear what to do.

To take care of your team, make sure each member feels well trained for his or her position and well treated. Give employees recognition for a job well done so they feel valued for their contribution. Whatever training, guidelines, or other good treatment you provide, the approach works because then team members feel good about themselves, their team, the company, and what they are doing. They can then better focus their attention on pleasing customers and adding value to their roles in the organization.

Work groups that consistently provide top-notch customer service share these common elements. They:
- Are well trained
- Are adequately staffed
- Clearly understand company policy
- Take pride in the company and its products and services
- Are self-critical and proactive in providing top-notice service, such as by holding regular staff meetings on how to offer better customer service and better respond to customer complaints
- Are given recognition, incentives, and bonuses for providing outstanding customer service
- Are led by a management team that has a vision and communicates that vision
- Are led by a management team that is a walking, talking role model of customer service
- Are treated as *internal customers* by management
- Are treated as *internal customers* by co-workers
- Are given information on what to do in response to likely problem situations, so they know their level of authority and empowerment.

If you can promote all these elements in your work groups, this powerful combination of traits will help strengthen everyone in the group to better deal with their customers, whatever the circumstances.

Exercise 10: Putting It All Together: Rating Yourself and Your Team on the Seven Essential Attitudes

The following exercise will help you assess your own and your team's level of development. Take the test individually and then combine your individual scores to get a group average. Or you can simply compare and discuss them. As you go through the following seven attitudes, rate yourself, your department, and your company on a scale of 1 to 10, with 1 being very poor and 10 representing outstanding service. Make copies of this scale so you can do these ratings separately. You can also use this exercise individually or as a group over a period of time, say every month or two, so you can assess your progress.

Rating Yourself and Your Team on the Seven Essential Attitudes

Being <u>empathetic</u> and <u>other-centered</u>, so you can put yourself in the other person's shoes.

1   2   3   4   5   6   7   8   9   10

Being <u>improvement oriented</u>, so you are striving for continuous improvement, and unwilling to "rest on your laurels."

1   2   3   4   5   6   7   8   9   10

Having a <u>determination to please</u>, so you like to delight the customer and do the unexpected to achieve customer satisfaction.

1   2   3   4   5   6   7   8   9   10

Having a <u>positive attitude</u>, sporting a smile and an optimistic outlook.

1   2   3   4   5   6   7   8   9   10

Having a <u>curiosity and love of learning</u>, so you think "I'll find out," rather than "I don't know."

1   2   3   4   5   6   7   8   9   10

Having an <u>ability to anticipate and take initiative</u>, so you work to anticipate the customer's likely questions and prepare in advance to answer them.

1   2   3   4   5   6   7   8   9   10

<u>Create an enviroment of team care</u>, so you are a good team player, eager and able to take good care of others on your customer service team.

1   2   3   4   5   6   7   8   9   10

How Did You Do?

Carefully review your results. You should be able to identify areas of strength and areas to improve upon. Don't ignore any of the data. It is all too easy to forget about the areas of strength, those areas you identified as 8-10 because, after all, you're already good in those areas, so why spend more time on them? Areas that are hovering in the range of 1-3 may seem too challenging to tackle. So, please don't fall into the trap of what I call the "comfort of neutrality." In other words, focusing on the areas that fall nicely into the 4-7 range—they aren't too weak to bother tweaking and they are strong enough to keep functioning at an acceptable level. You need to bring the lower scores up, because they will usually become the weak link in the long chain of service and leadership. For example, if you do everything else, but don't strive for continuous improvement, attitude #2, eventually you'll fall behind and all the smiles in the world won't make up for your lack of knowledge, or outdated products and services. Likewise, if you don't have a positive attitude and smile, attitude #4, it doesn't matter if you are trying very hard to be an empathetic, curious, and committed team player. Your lack of a warm, positive nature will turn off customers as well as other employees.

Work on correcting any traits where you fall behind and vow to continue supporting the traits where you already demonstrate strength. Then, as you bring that lower scoring trait up to speed, your whole performance will improve dramatically. It's like the Olympian high-jumper who has an injured heel in a cast and can't get over the bar. She's great in every other respect, but that injured foot keeps her securely on the ground. Once her foot is healed and the cast comes off, watch how she soars. Think of yourself and your team at work as a team of Olympians. Work on polishing up those seven attitudes and have them all at the highest level—then watch how you soar.

A Final Word

Let's not forget the fundamental message of this book: to maintain a balance in your approach to service, both with your internal and external customers. Hopefully, as you read this book and participated in the exercises, you kept in mind the proverb *Even monkeys fall from trees*. Ideally, you reflected on how you and your team members, the management, and company employees typically have responded to situations when you "fell from the customer service tree" and had to engage in damage control activities. Throughout the book, I challenged you to take one of two paths:

A. You can stay on the ground after that. Blame others for your fall. Never admit the problems. Never recover from the fall. Or,

B. You can leap back up to the tree by admitting the problems and using feedback from customers and co-workers to keep you in balance out on those limbs.

I firmly believe that you can stay up in the tree even longer if you are honest and admit to yourself what strength and areas of improvement you have. The journey of excellent service and leadership can be a challenge you choose to accept or reject. The question, once again, is:

The choice is yours, which path will you take?

About the Author

Douglas Lipp, MA, is the founder and president of G. Douglas Lipp & Associates. The consulting and training services offered by his firm are designed to help organizations examine their management styles and strategies, then determine the effectiveness of each with respect to providing outstanding leadership and service. Much of his work is focused on how organizations and individuals can excel in the ever-changing global marketplace.

Formerly with the Walt Disney Company and NEC Electronics, Doug has spent over 20 years working from the front lines to the boardrooms of corporations around the world.

At Disney, Doug worked as a trainer at the Disney University at Disneyland in Anaheim, where he taught the well-known "Traditions" orientation program and many leadership courses. Doug was also chosen to be a member of the start-up team for Tokyo Disneyland, and was transferred to Japan for two years during the project. Upon his return to the U.S., he became the head of training at the Disney Studios.

As a much sought after consultant, trainer and speaker, Doug now helps audiences around the world understand the Disney magic by taking them "behind the scenes" to discover the secret of this success. His humorous and down-to-earth style has attracted a wide variety of organizations and industries including: Motorola, GE Capital, Universal Studios, NEC Electronics, Pebble Beach Resorts, Bell Mobility Cellular, Northstar-At-Tahoe, Merrill Lynch, Boise Cascade, Macy's, IBM, ADAC Labs, Accenture (formerly

Andersen Consulting), U.S. Postal Service, Conseco Fund Group, Paramount, University of California, Veterans' Health Administration, Toshiba America and Wells Fargo Bank.

He is the author of *Tokyo Disneyland: The Secret of Its Success*; *Danger & Opportunity: Resolving Conflict in U.S.-Based Japanese Subsidiaries*; and *Global Management*.

For more information about Doug's presentations, training, consulting or to order more books, visit his website at **www.douglipp.com** or email him at doug@douglipp.com.